GREAT FIGHTER JETS
OF THE
GALAXY 1

First edition Fall 2021
King Tiger Books
www.kingtigerbooks.com

ISBN 978-0-9781129-5-0

This book contains artwork based on the novels published by King Tiger Books, a small printshop specializing in fantasy and science fiction where world building and imaginative settings come first. King Tiger Books started off as a dream about books where the creative world building part continued right up to the end. I have personally read over 5,000 fantasy and science fiction novels and found many of them conformed to the same pattern – 2 or 3 awesome chapters where the world was presented to the reader, exciting stuff where I could almost see the author's hand putting his chess pieces down in preparation for whatever fantasy or science fiction battles were to come.

The rest of the novels were often bland, non-descript and painfully filled with conversations. Sometimes the rest of the books had the characters walking around, like in one famous novel where a little halfling-person walked all the way across a dangerous fantasy world to throw his wedding ring into a volcano. The movie adaptation was good though.

King Tiger books did things differently. My brother and I worked out the plots to our books together, focusing on setting, environment and background and making sure that the entire novel was like the first 2 or 3 chapters from other novels that I loved so much. The result is a series of books that contain more world building in 1 chapter than many other books have in their entirety. Our first novel, War Machines of von Saarik, is illustrated here. I used a wonderful program called Vue 16 Esprit to bring the world of Imtrund to life, spending countless hours drawing the crystals, castles and magic swords so important to the book's plot.

Penturian, our second novel, gets royal treatment here. A neat blend of science fiction and fantasy, Penturian showcased a fighter pilot named Tychon of Kalos who fought valiantly at 20,000 feet to defend his planet from fire elementals, high tech ships and greedy old gods that wouldn't die.

The jets from many of our science fiction novels are here including the single seat ships that the Octopoid Empire used to explore the galaxy in Iliad 2030, an intoxicating mix of science fiction, aviation and world building. Achiliosa rampaged through the skies in that one, gunning her enemies down in battle after battle.

The jets from Star Pilot – a science fiction novel about defending civilized space from an intergalactic race of merciless reptiles – are here, boldly entering battle despite overwhelming odds. So grab some coffee, sit back and look through the pictures, exploring the galaxy along with my brave fighter pilots. Or pick up the books from King Tiger Books and read about their adventures, narrow escapes and epic battles.

– Tim Gibson 2021

GREAT JET FIGHTERS

OF THE

GALAXY 1

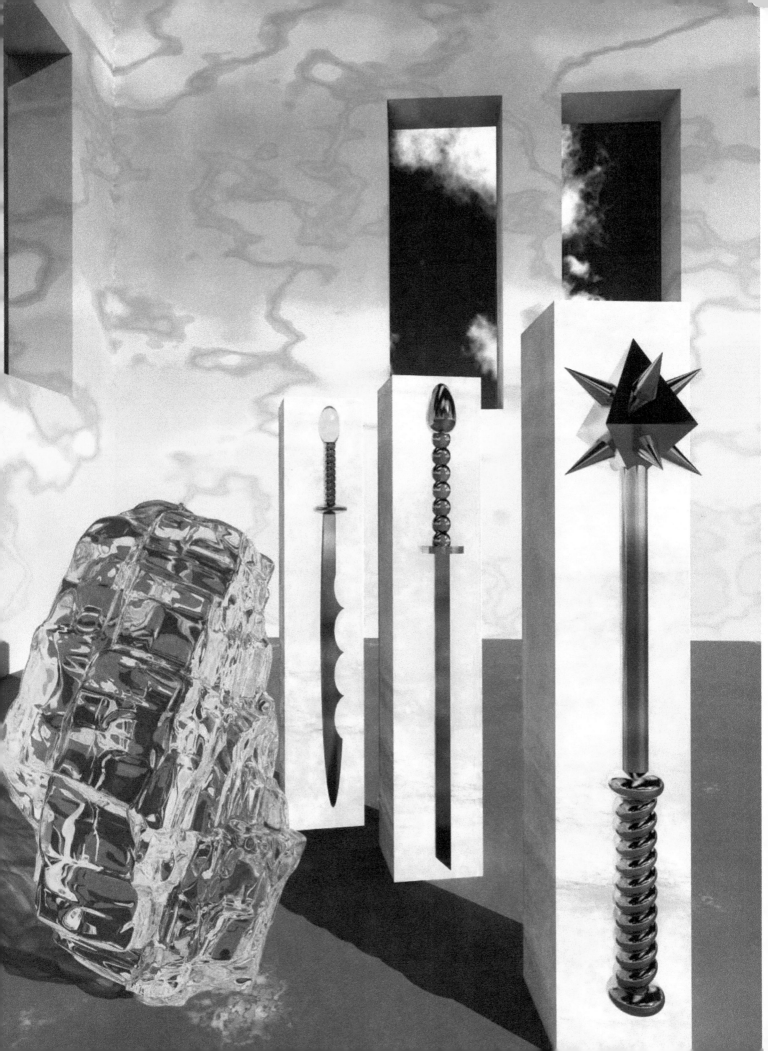

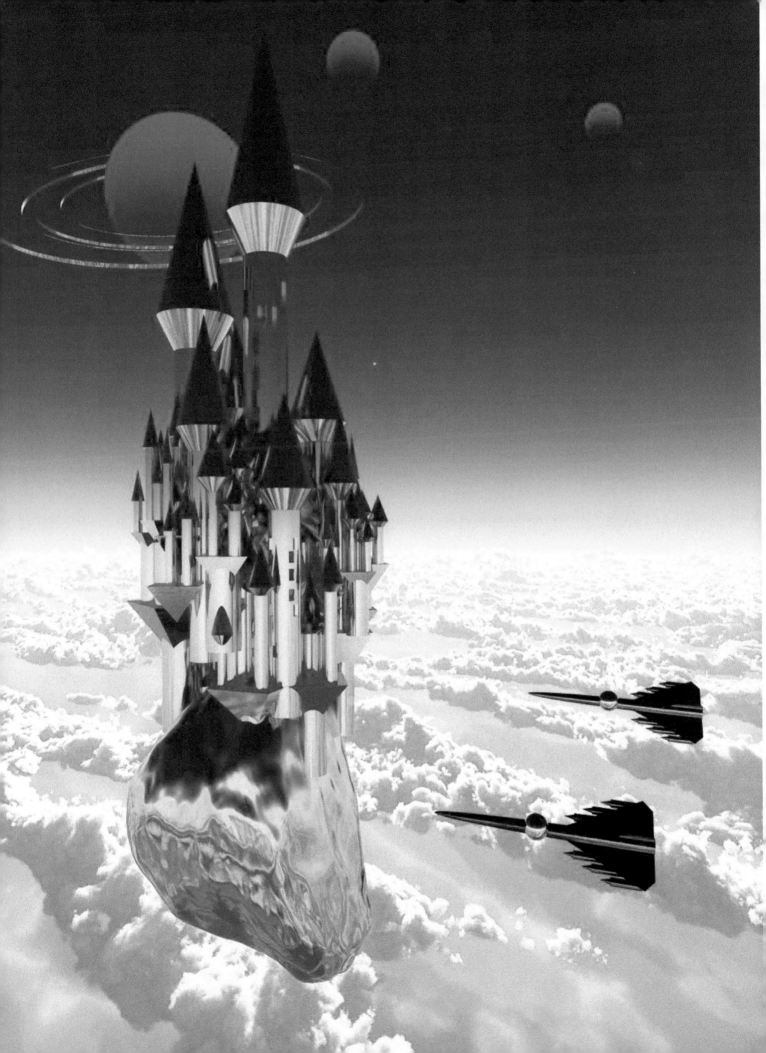

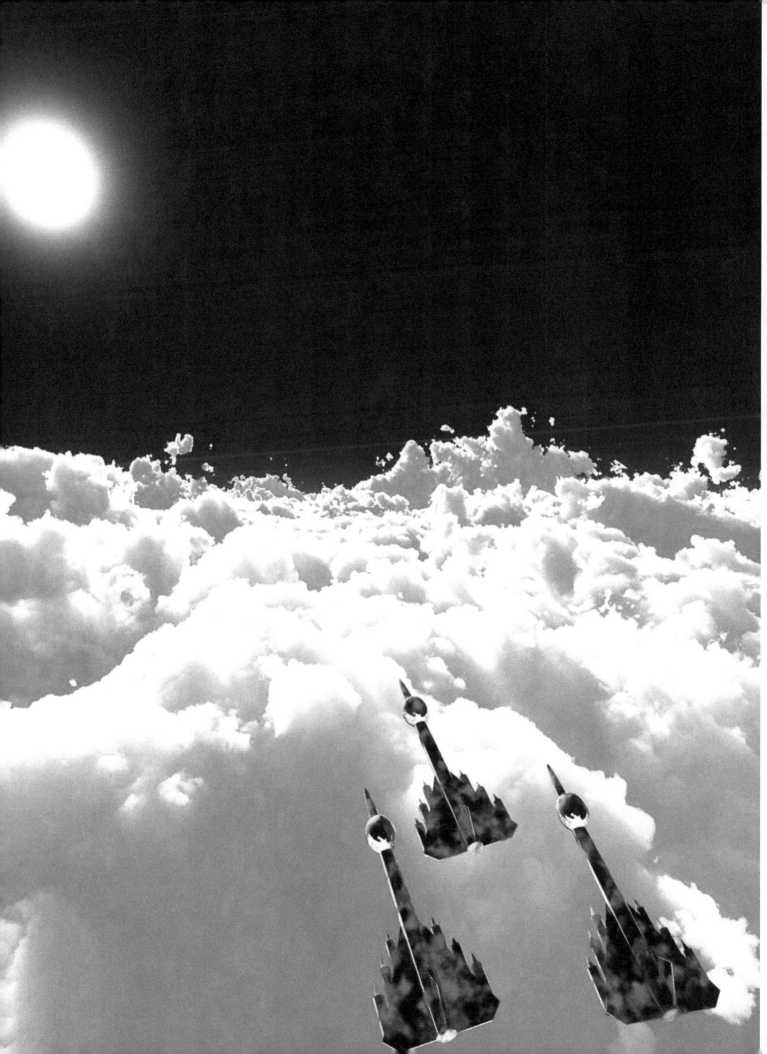

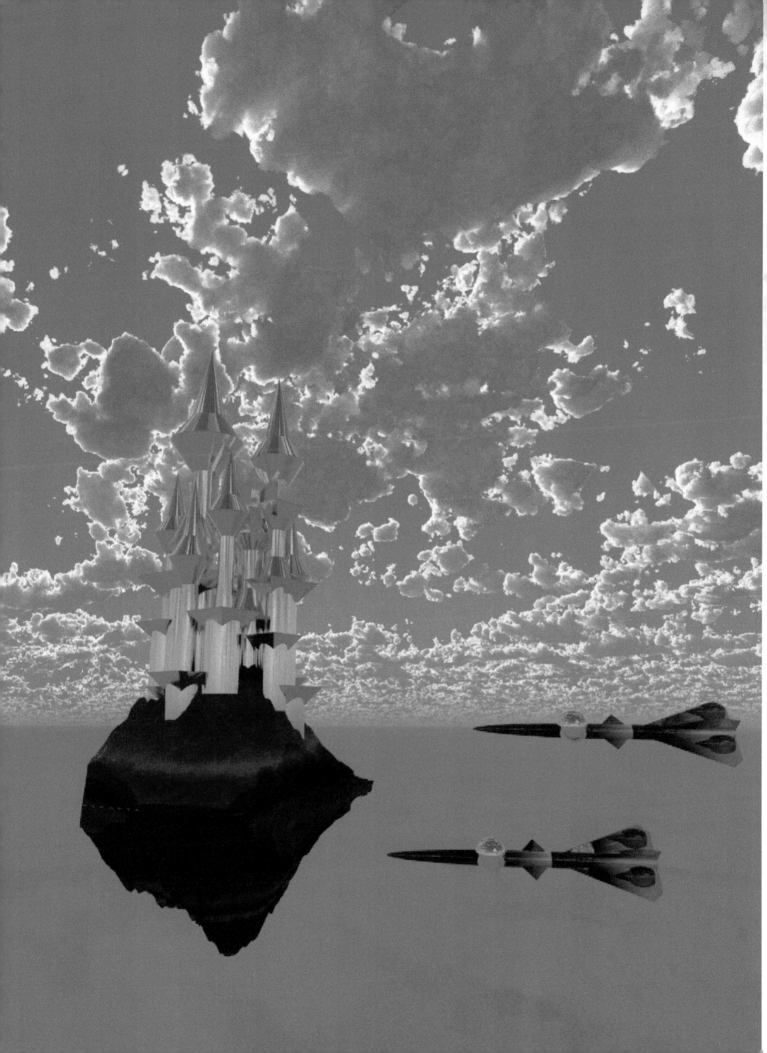

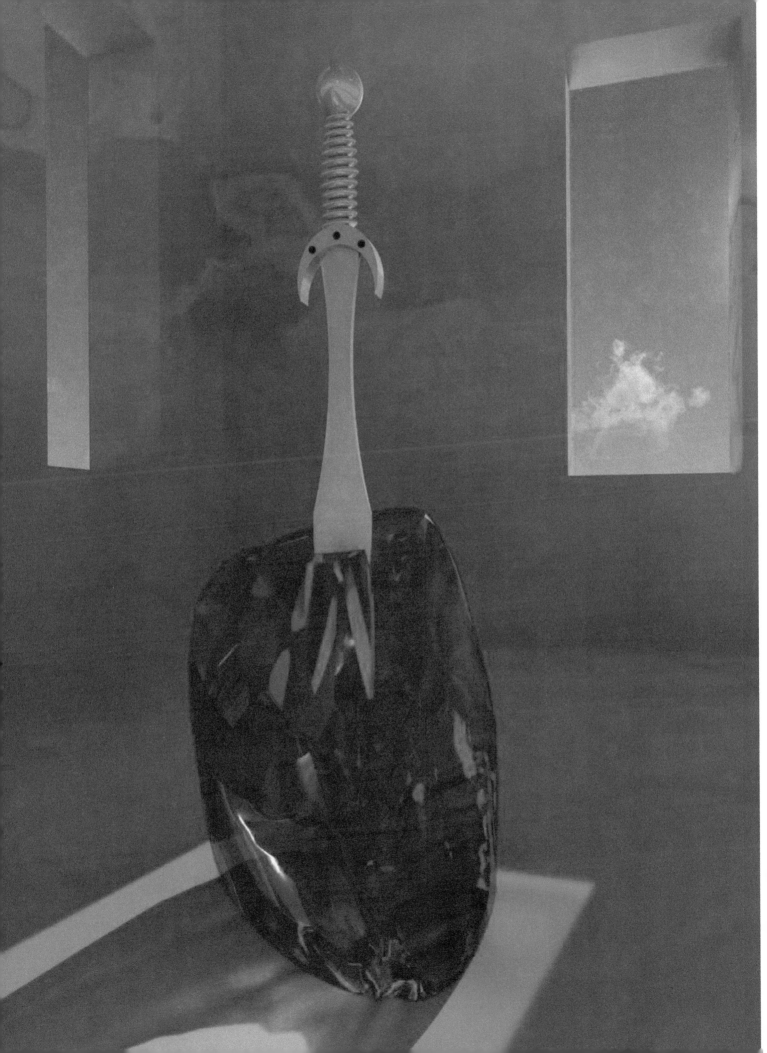

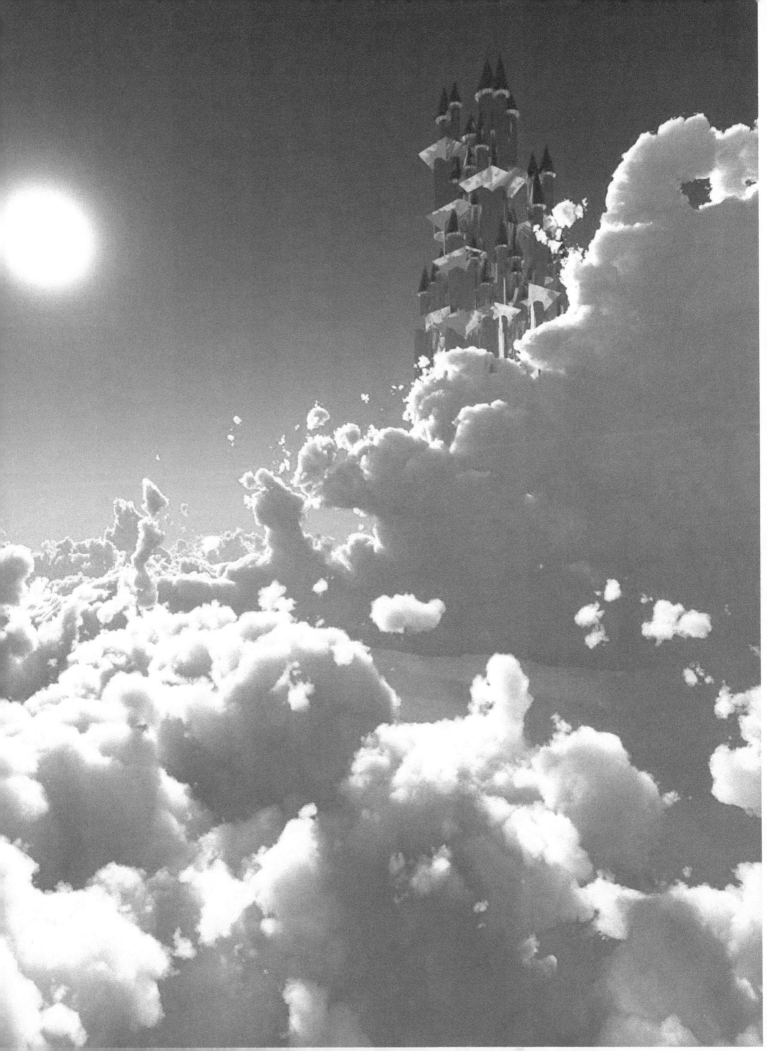

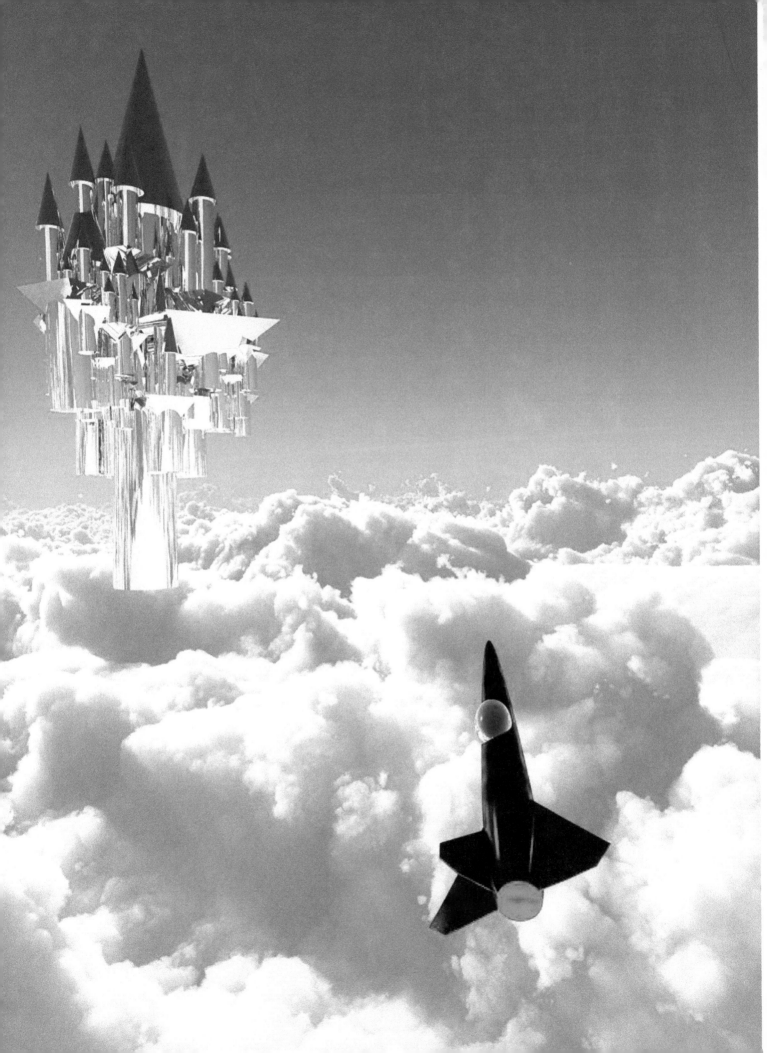

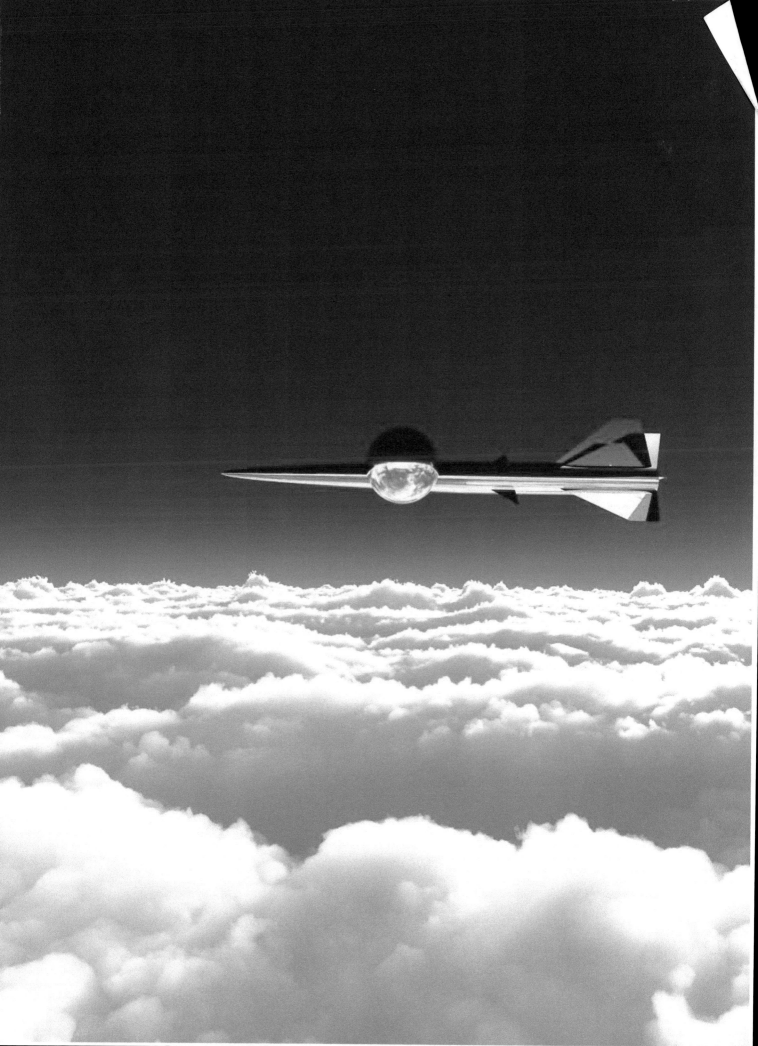

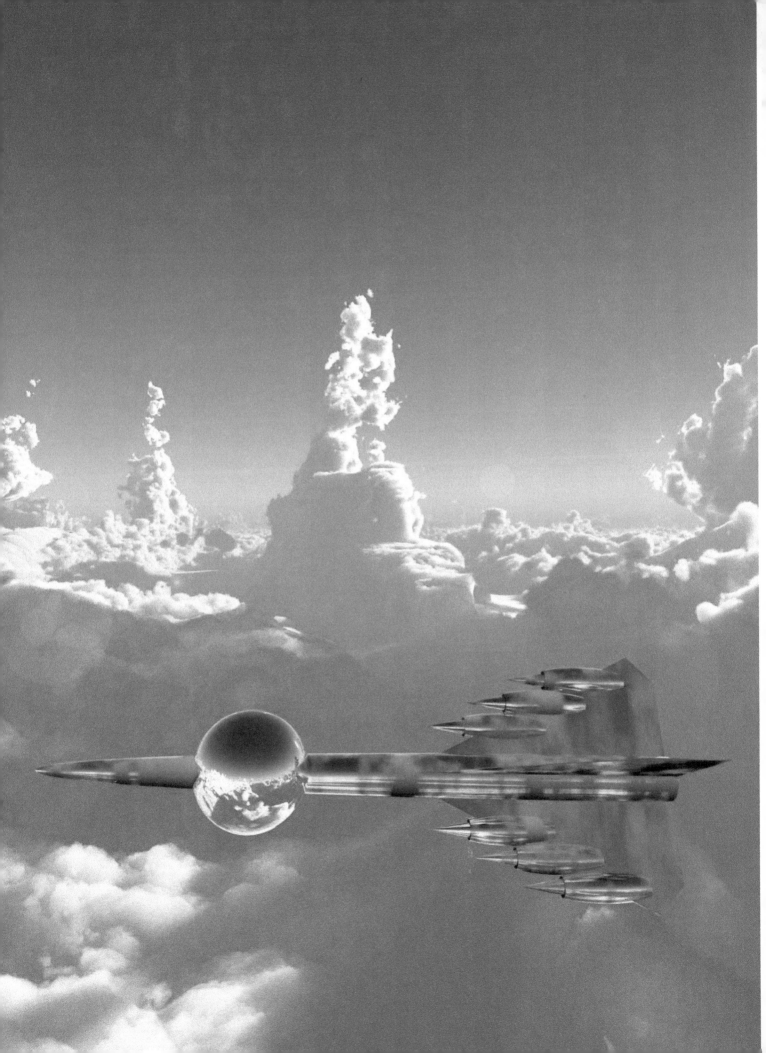

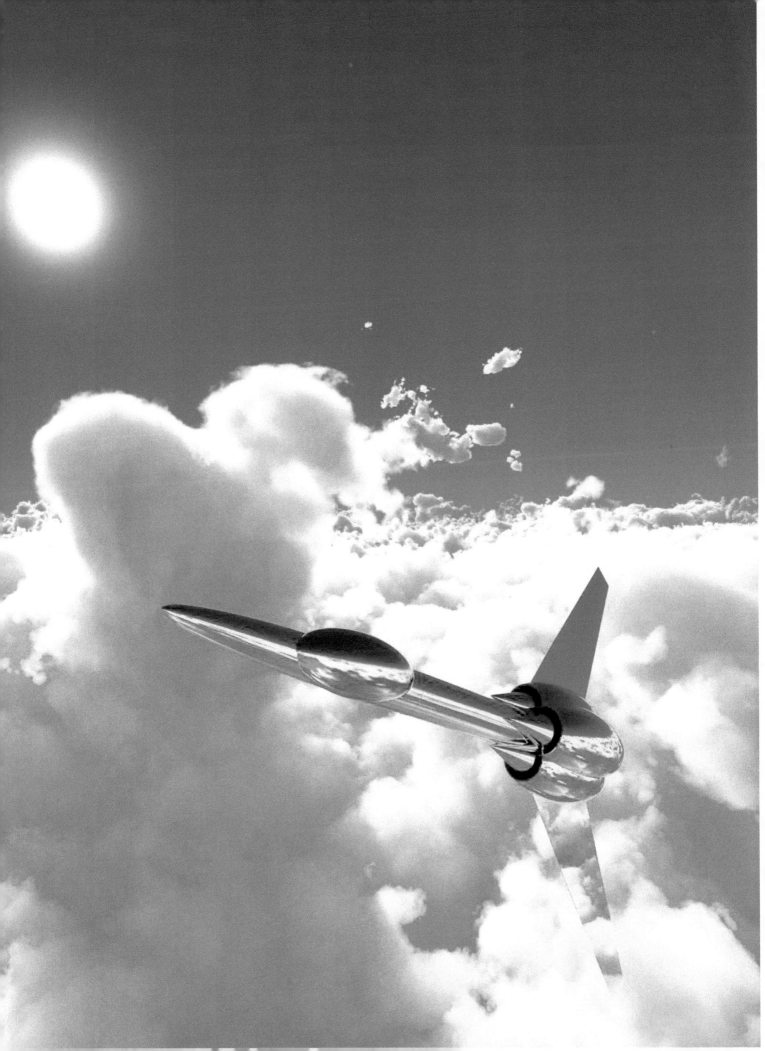

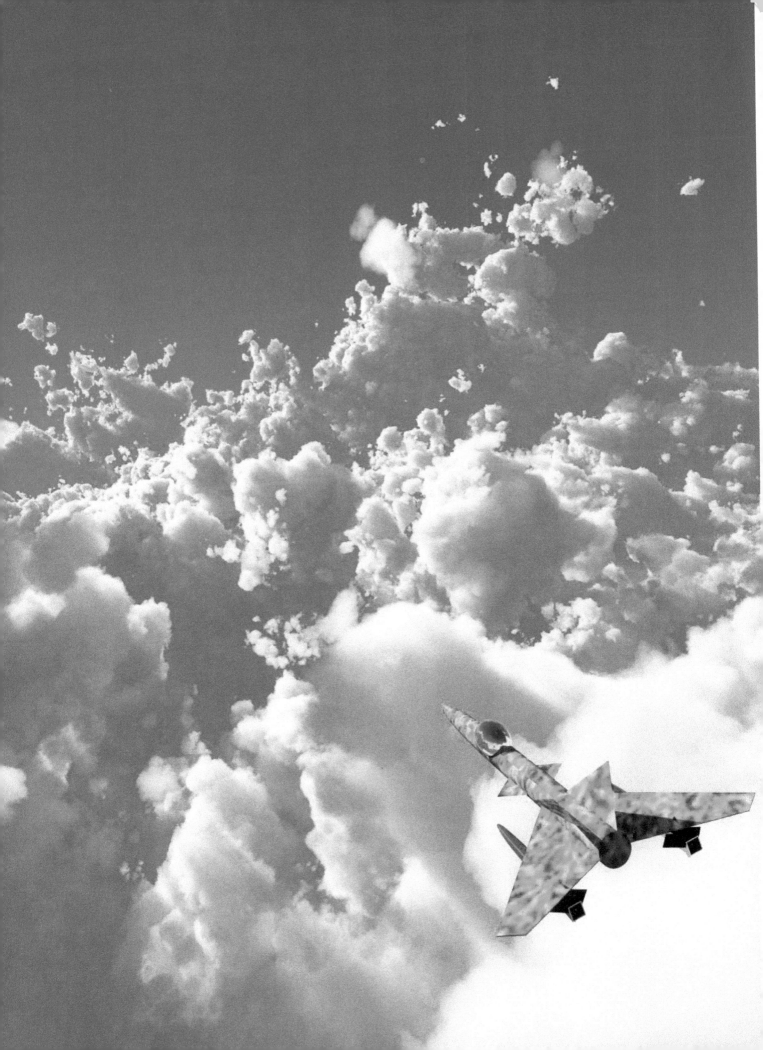

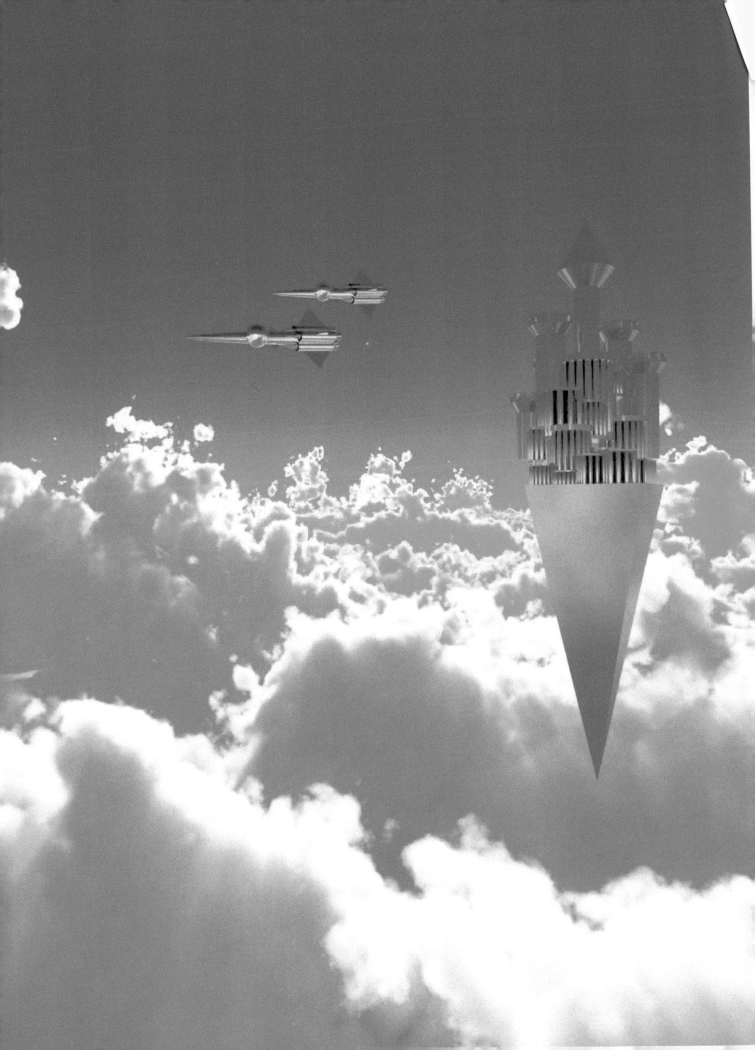

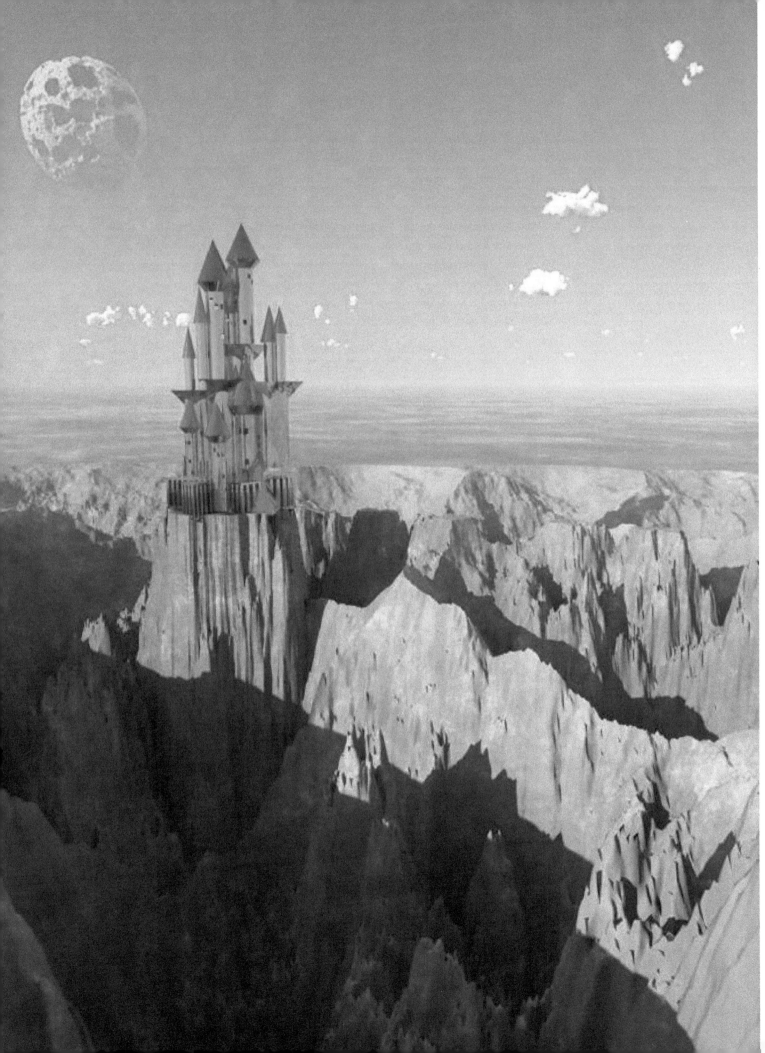

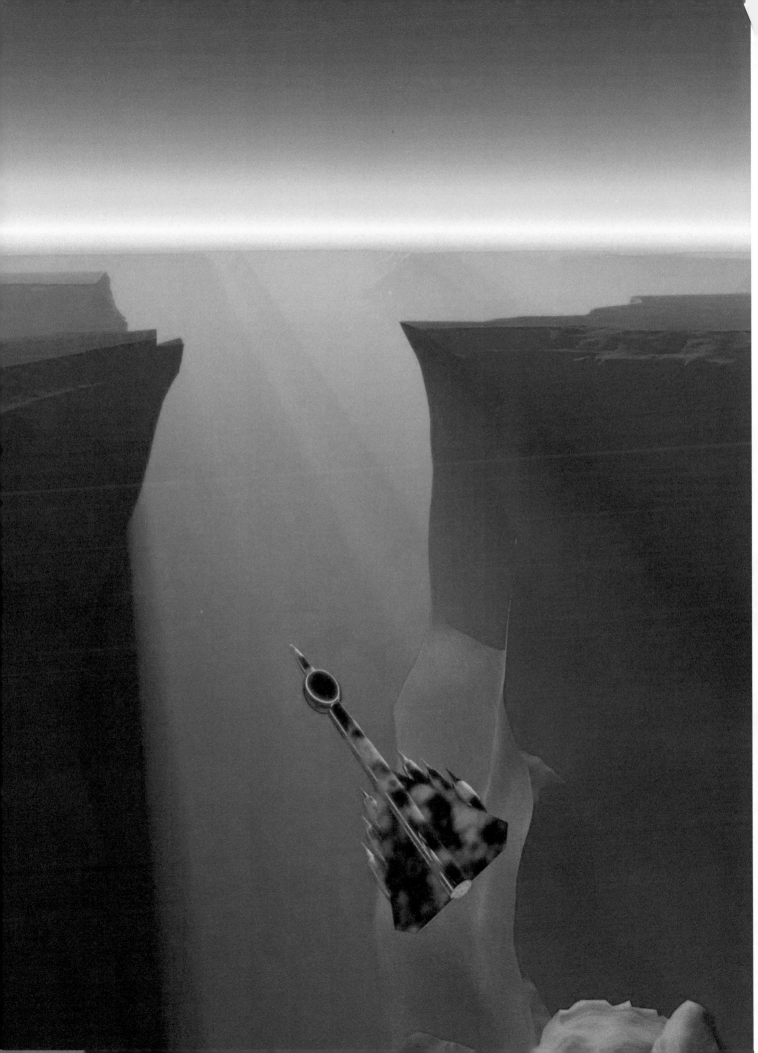

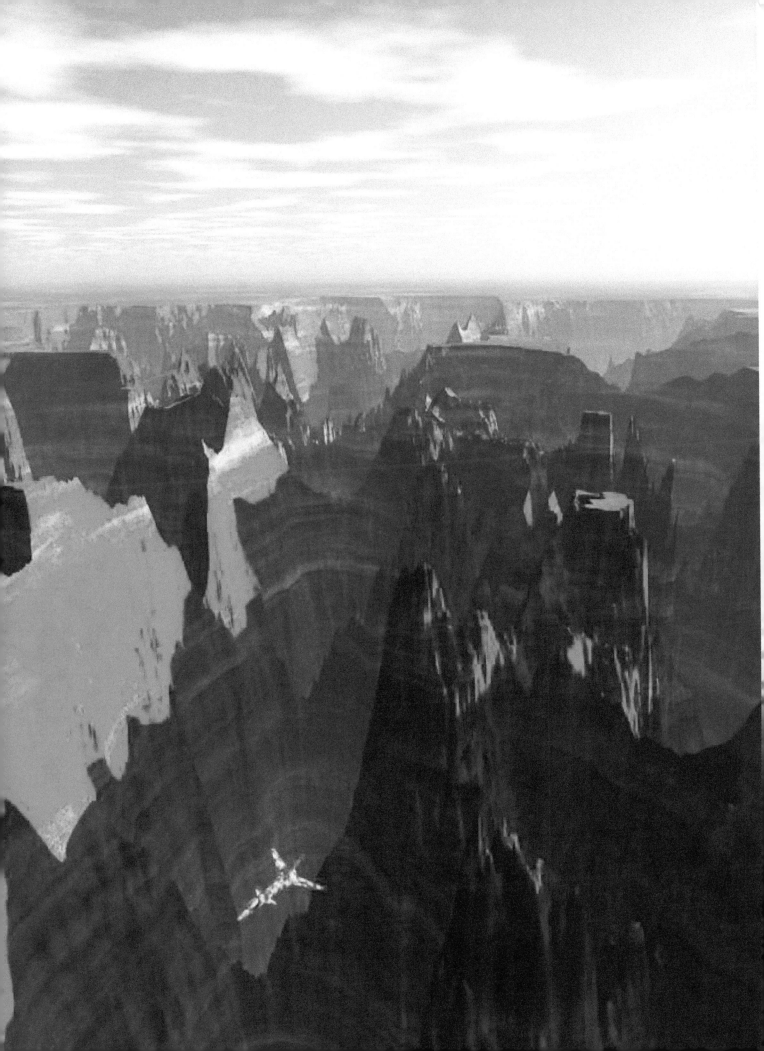

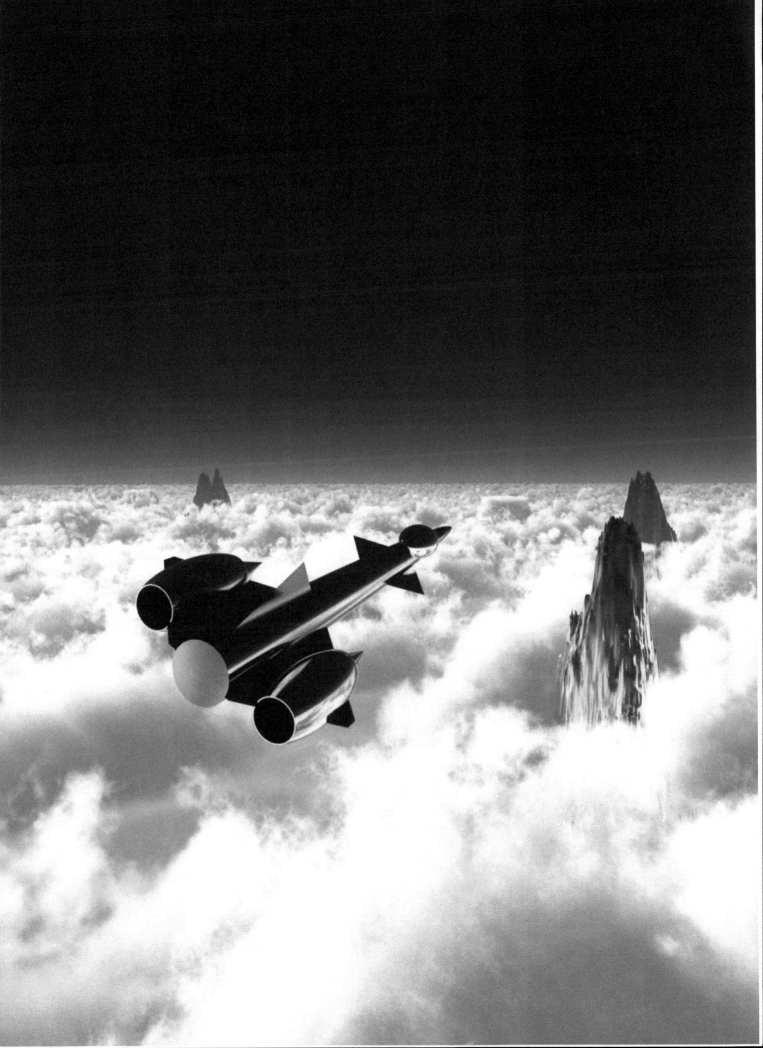

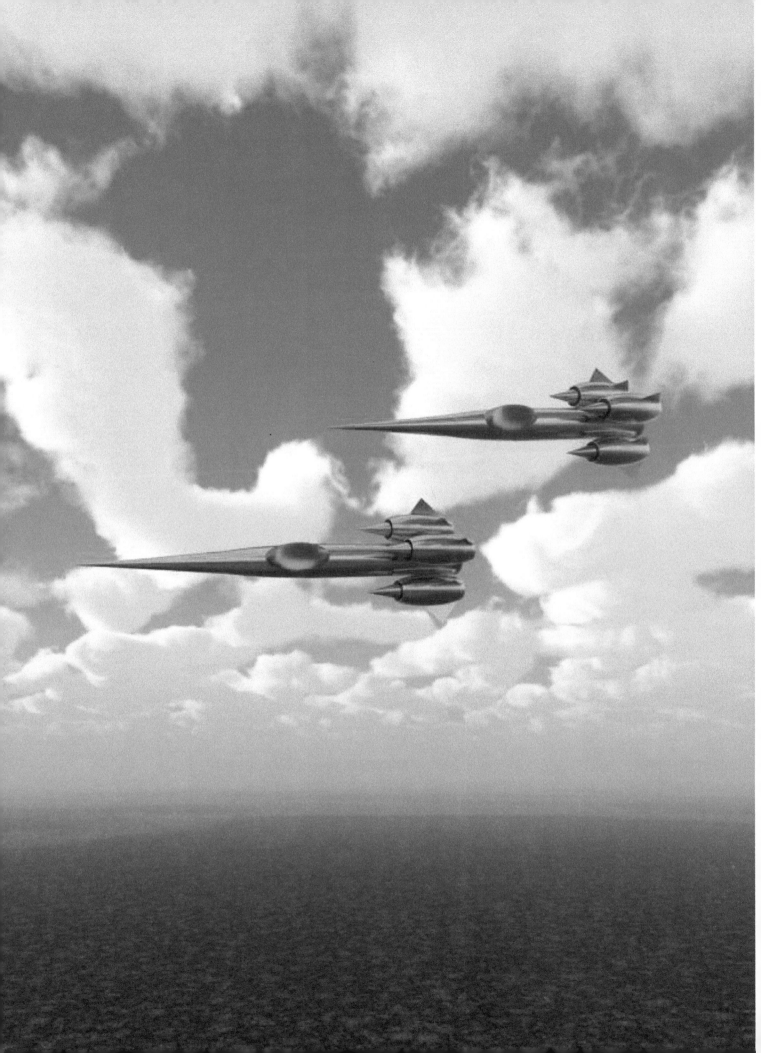

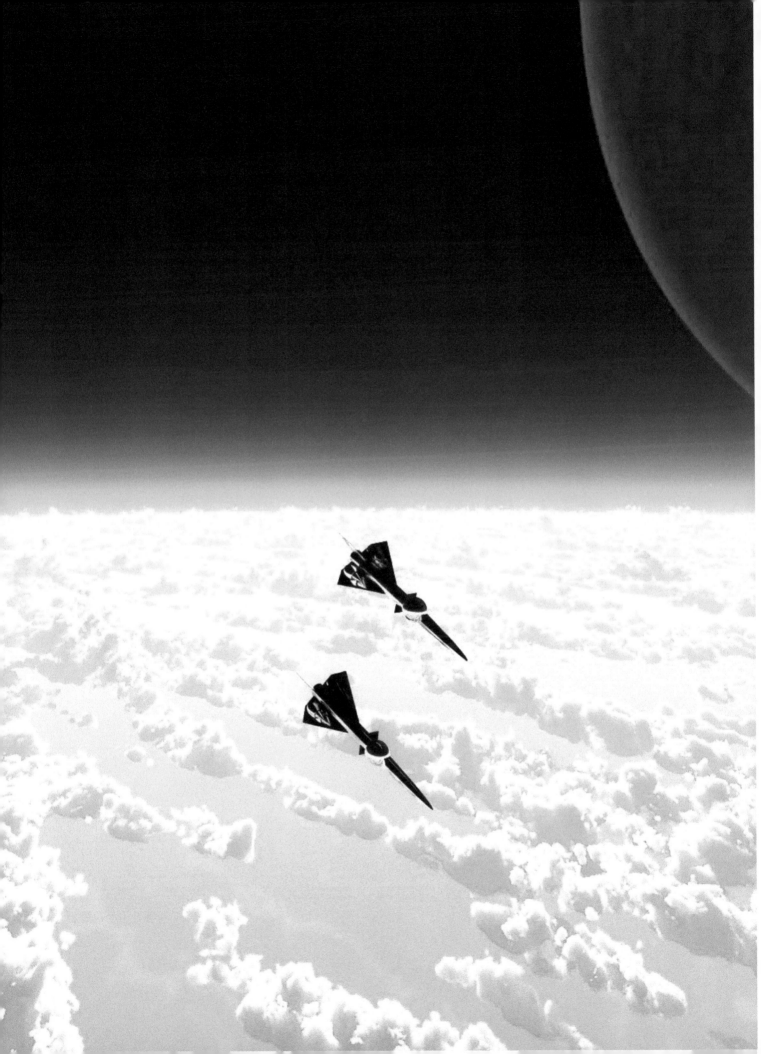

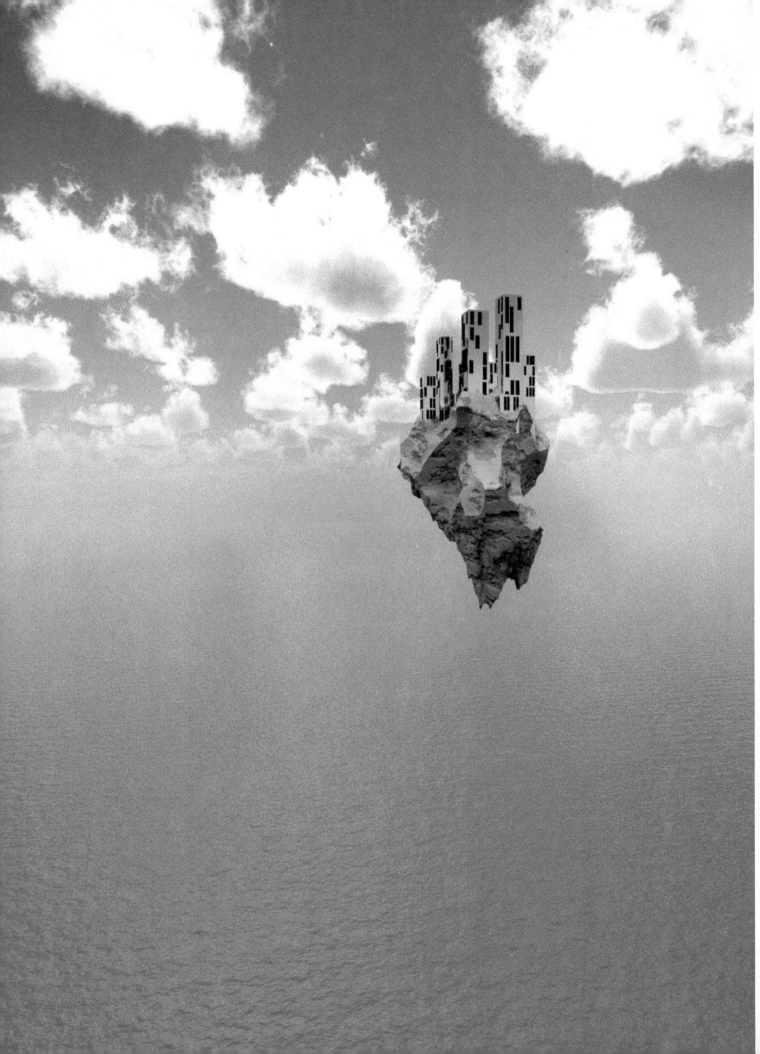

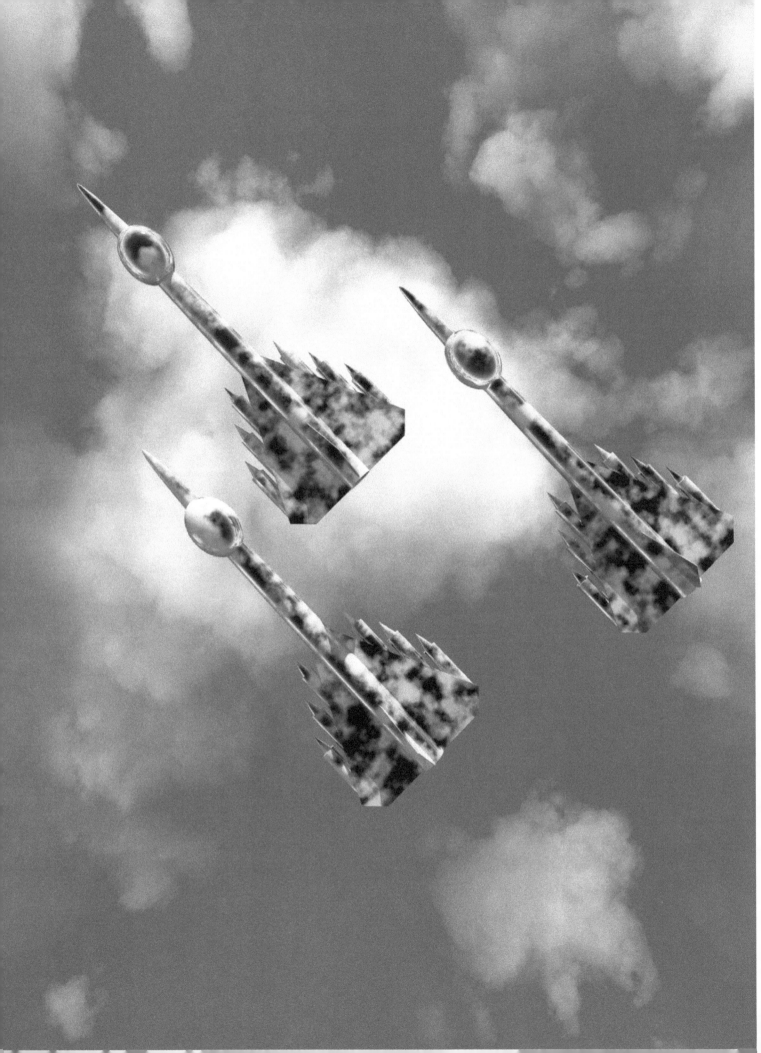

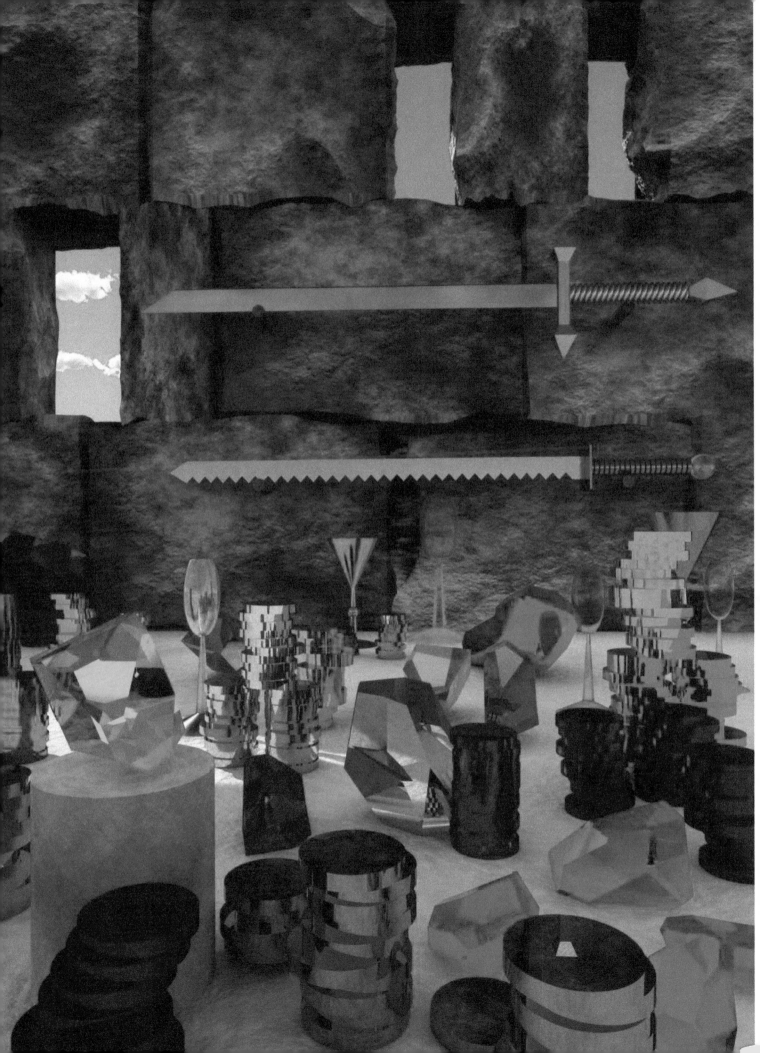

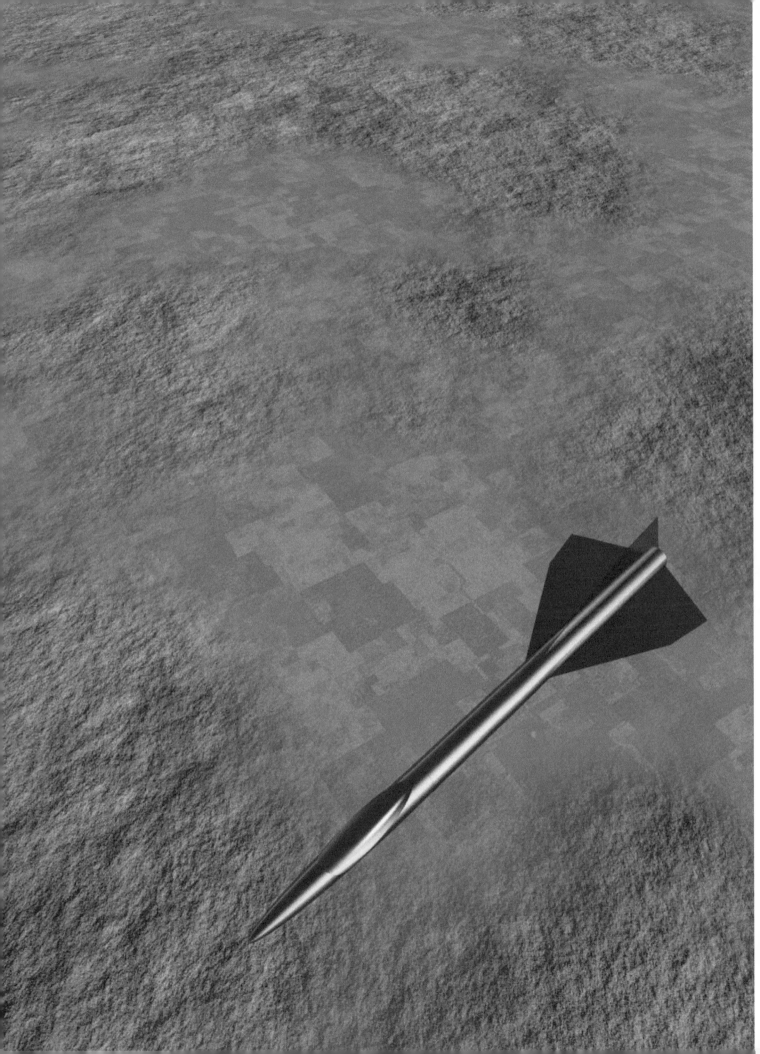

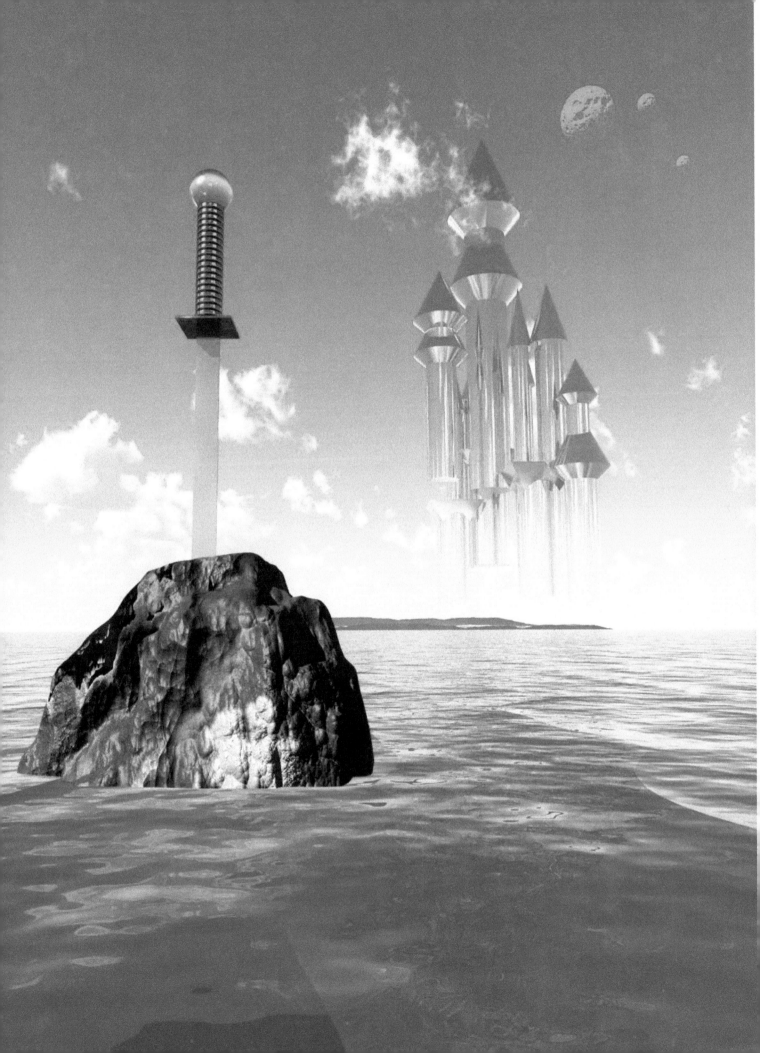

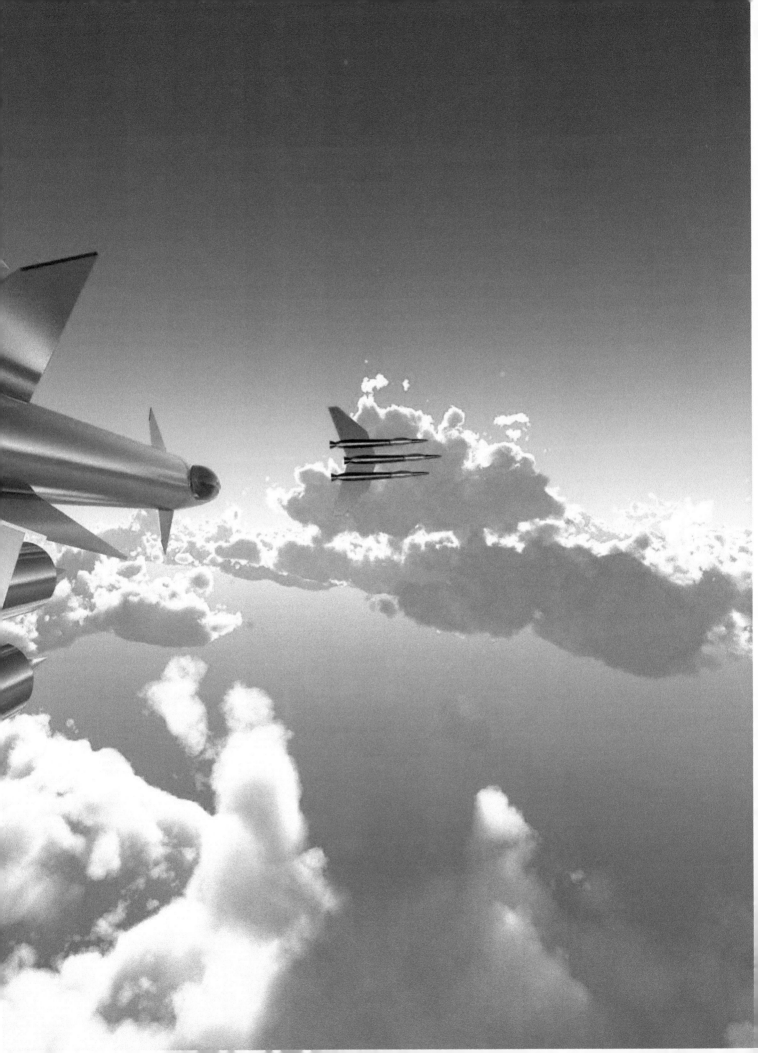

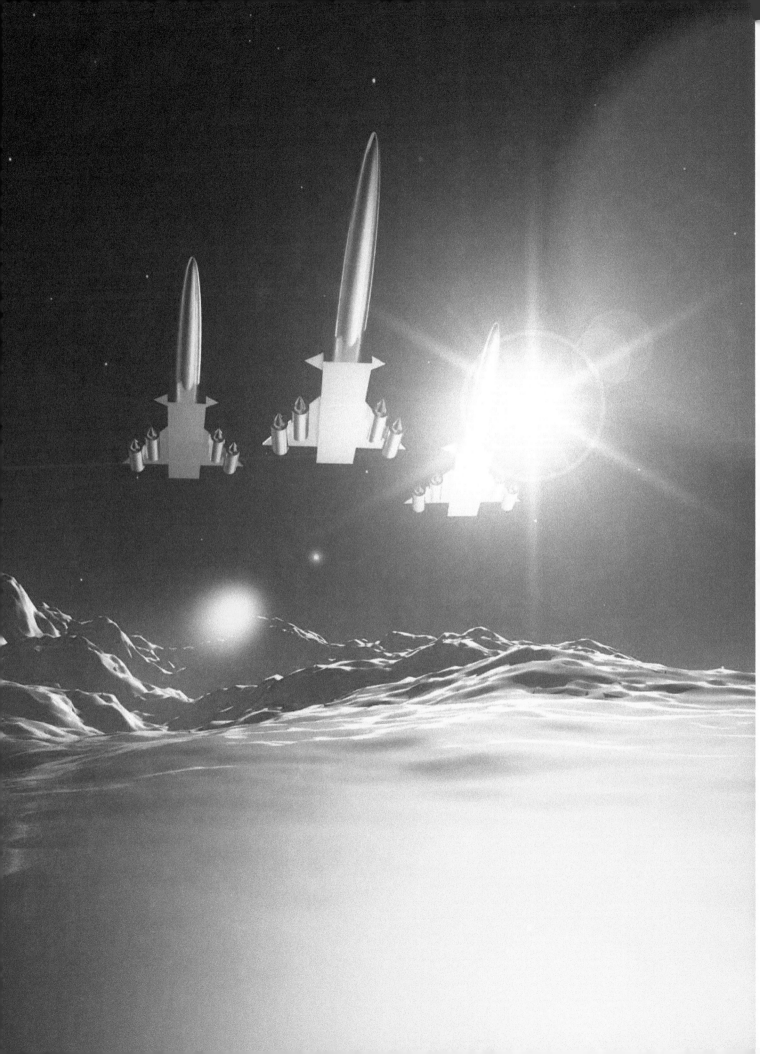

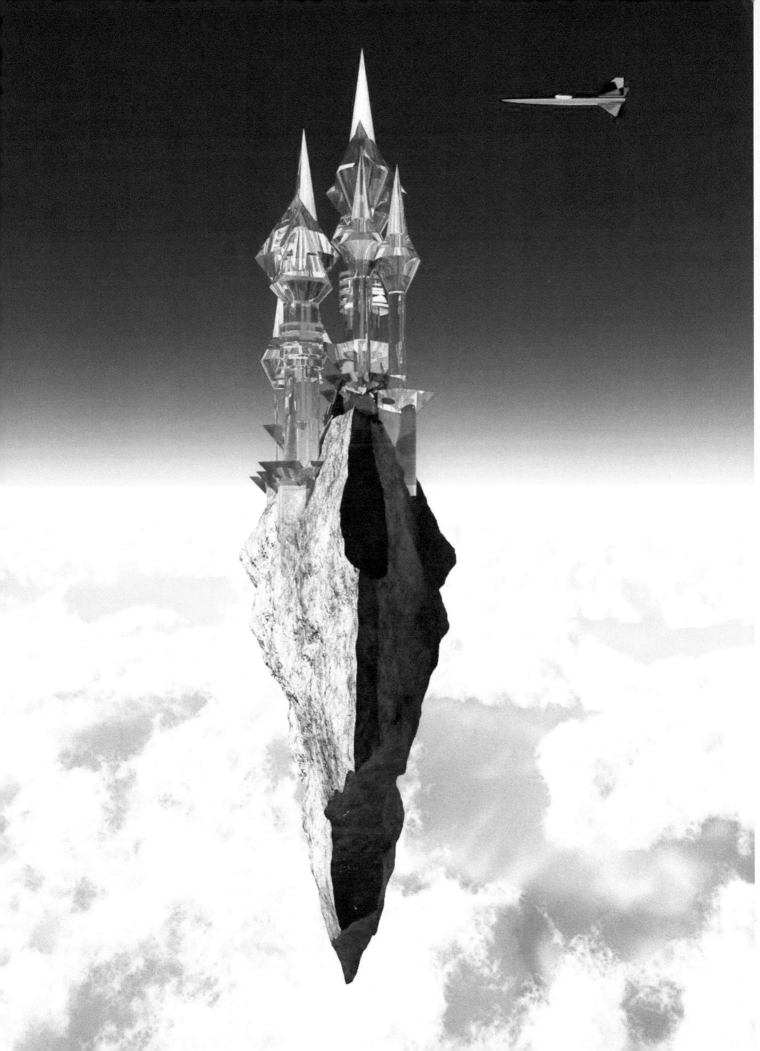

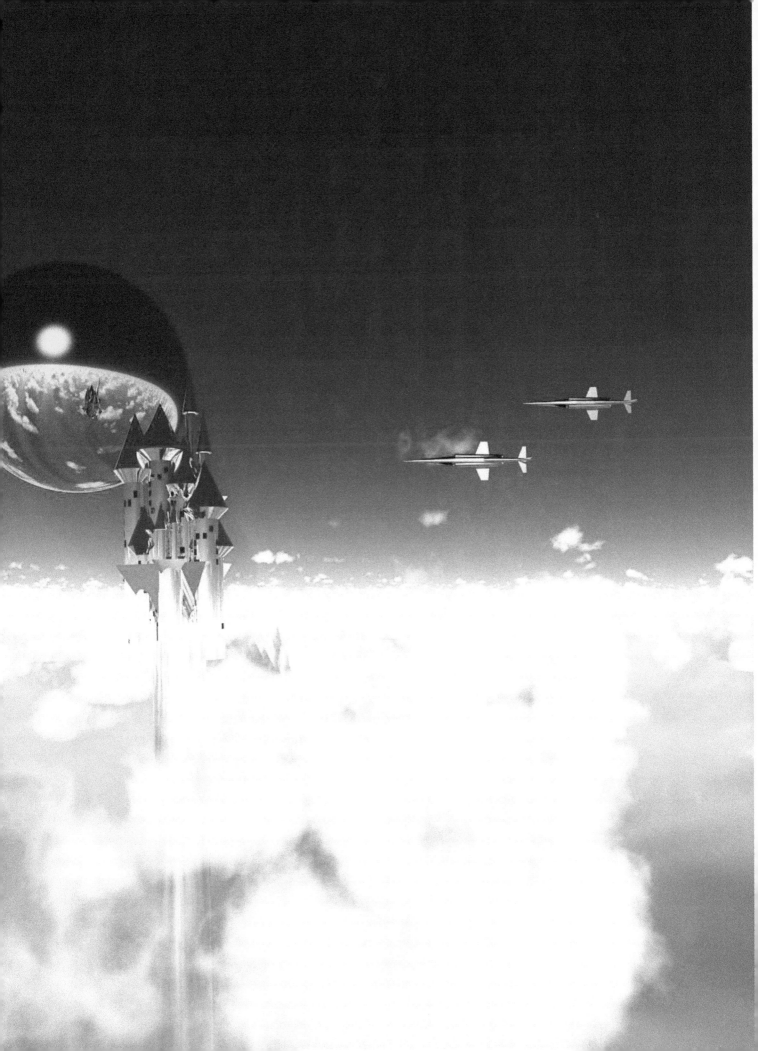

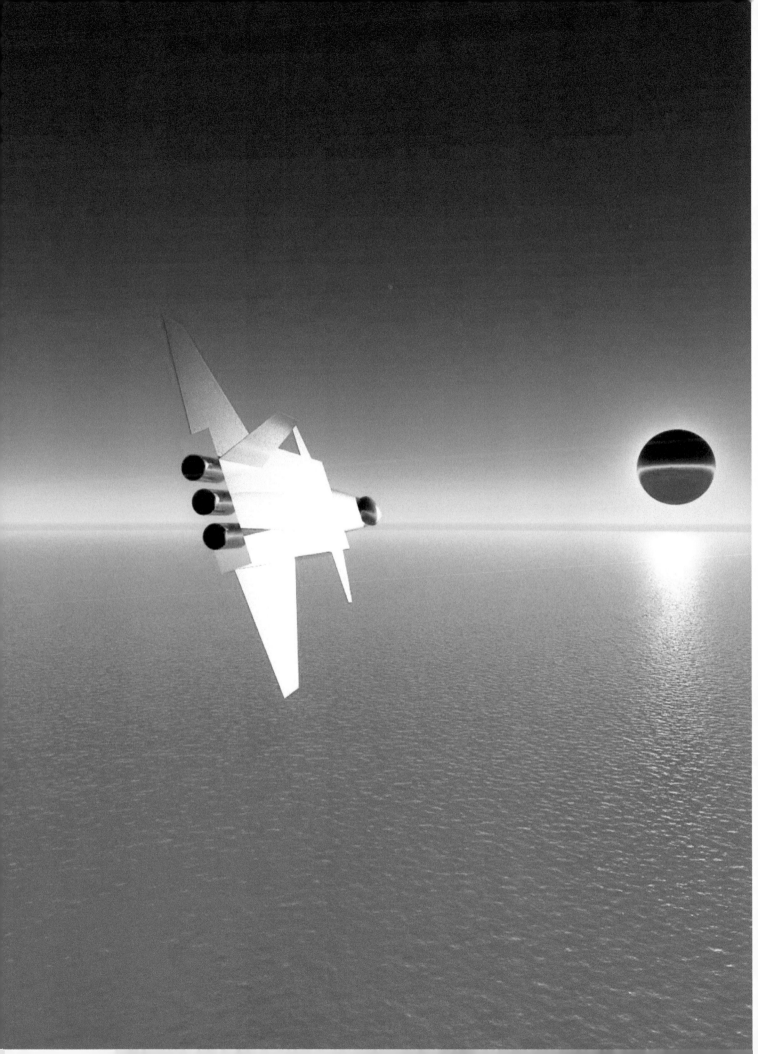

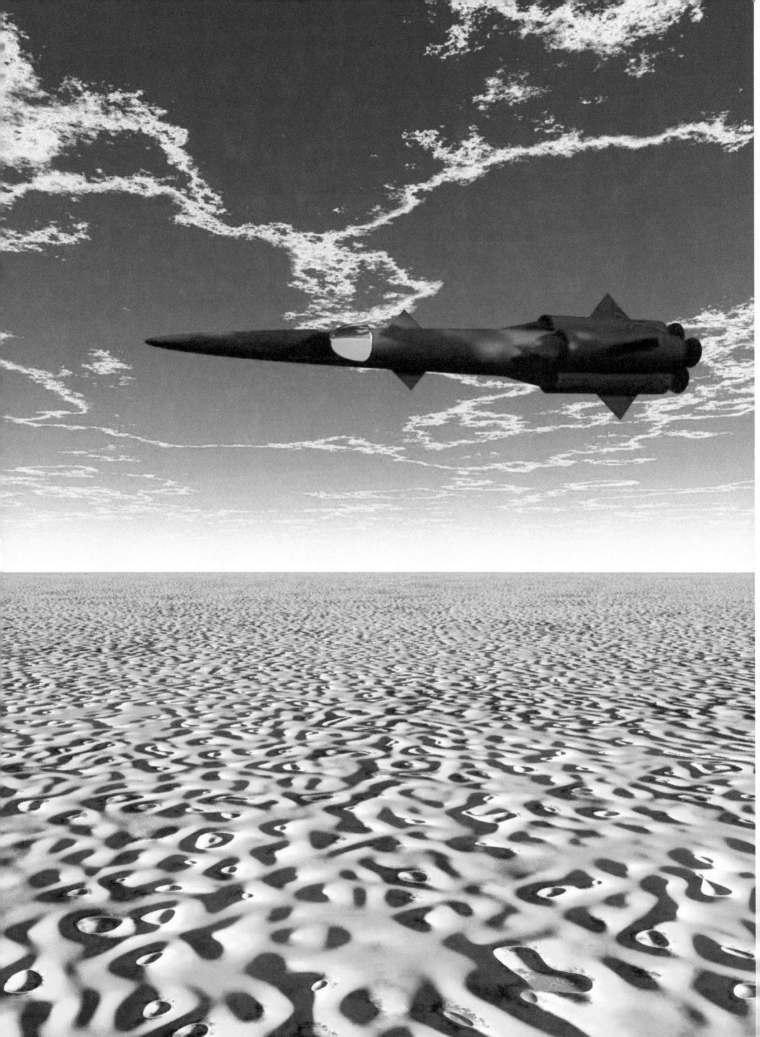

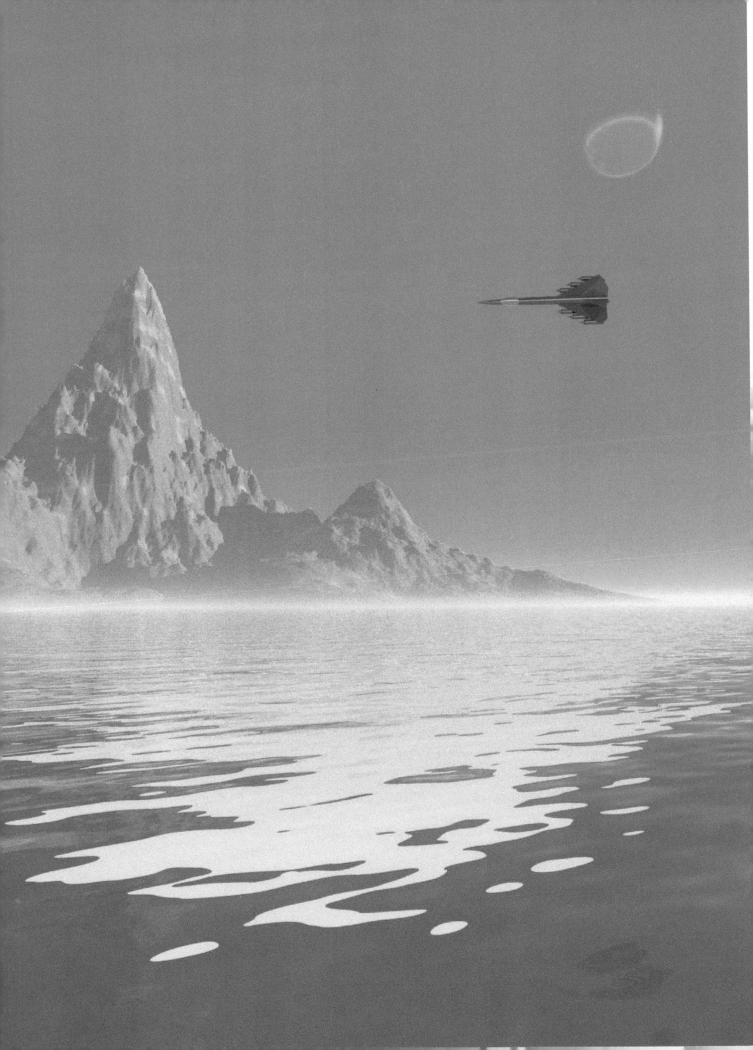

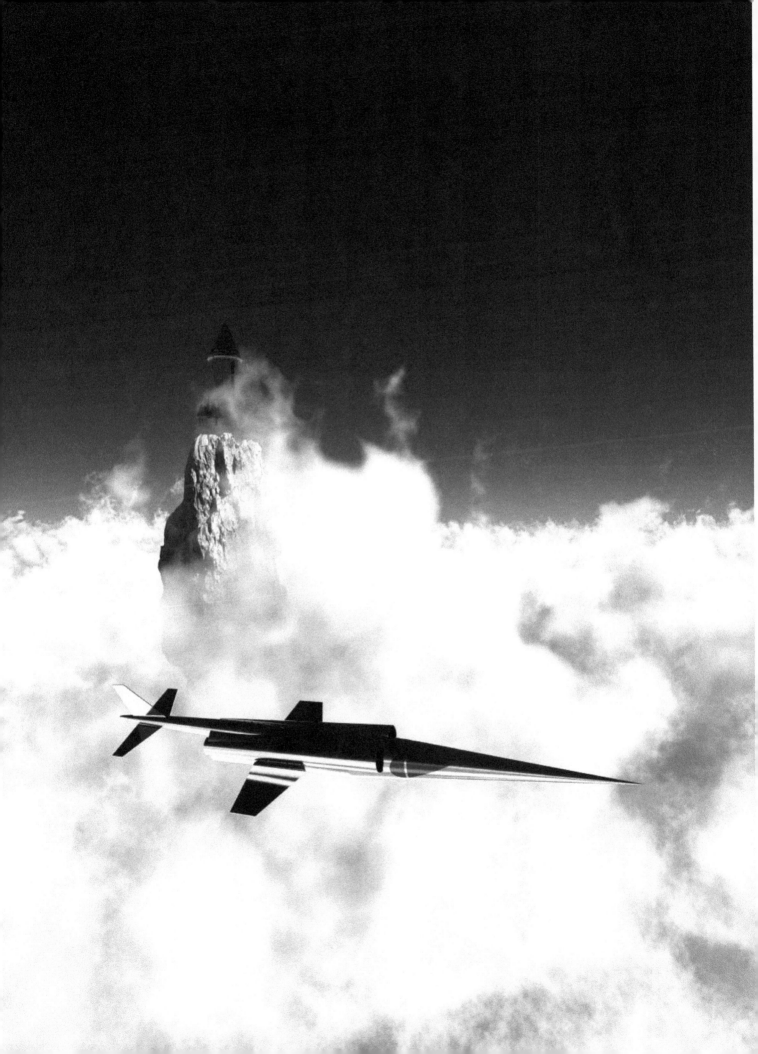

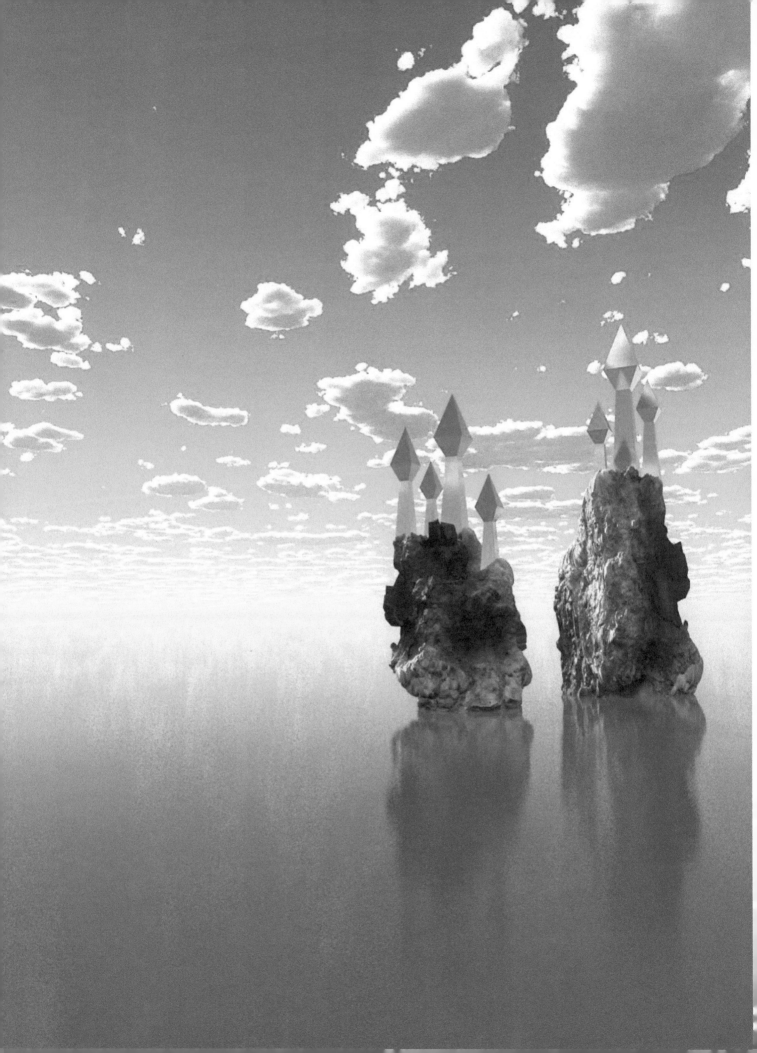

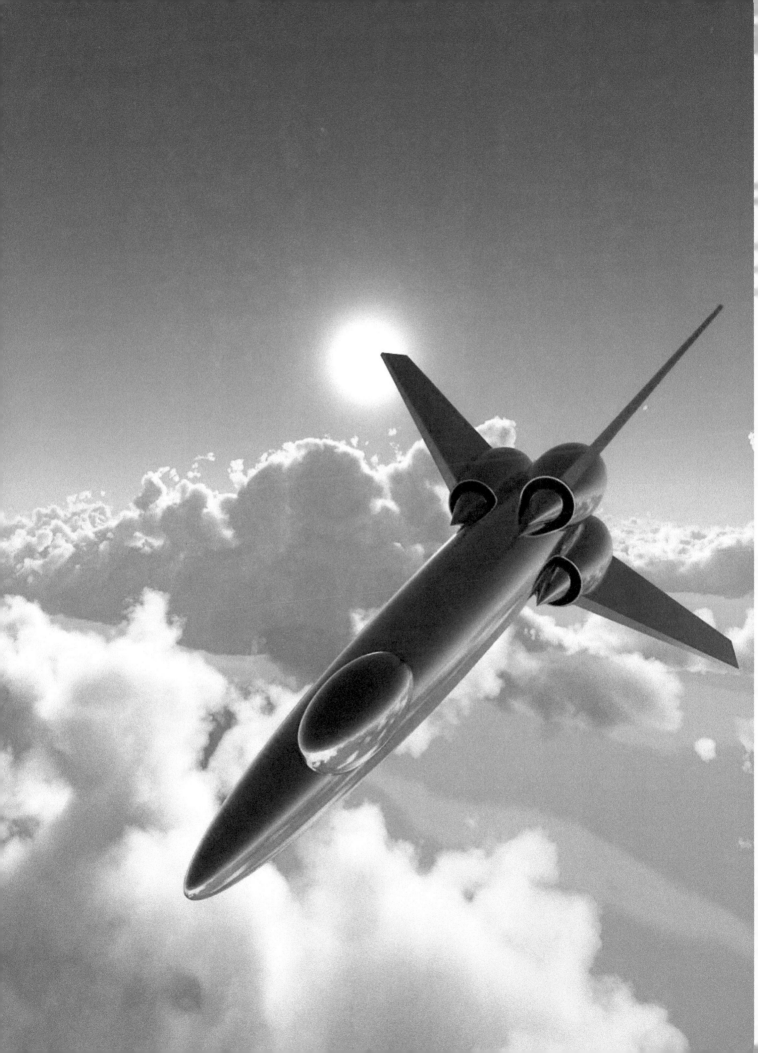

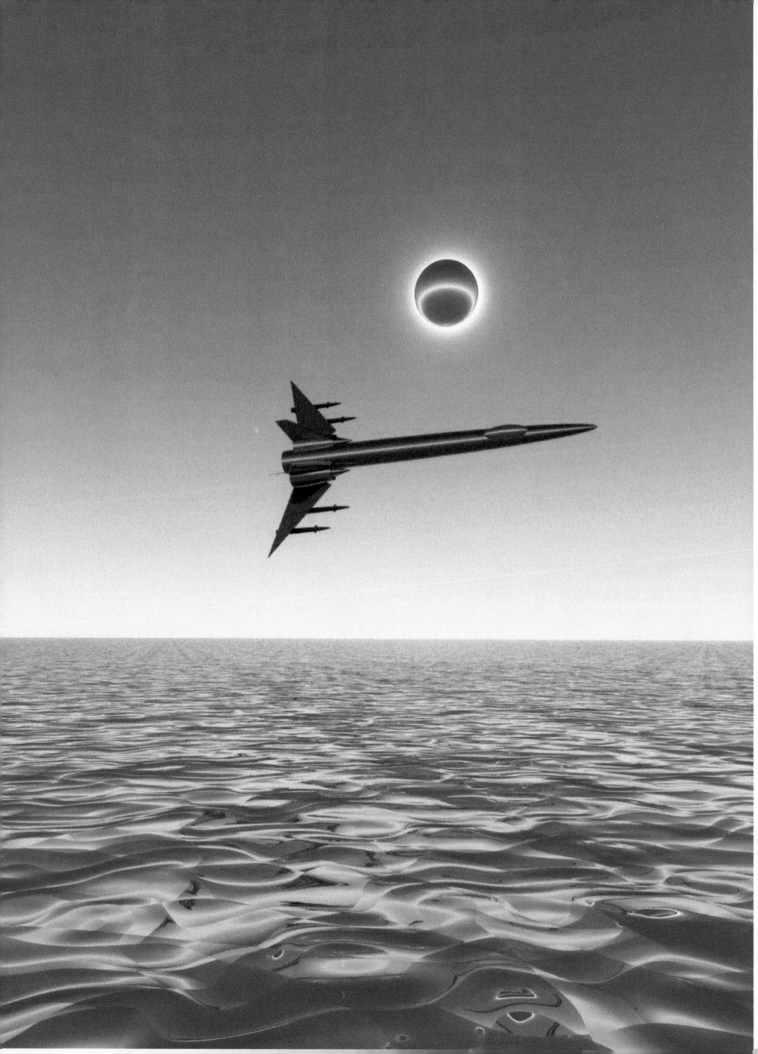

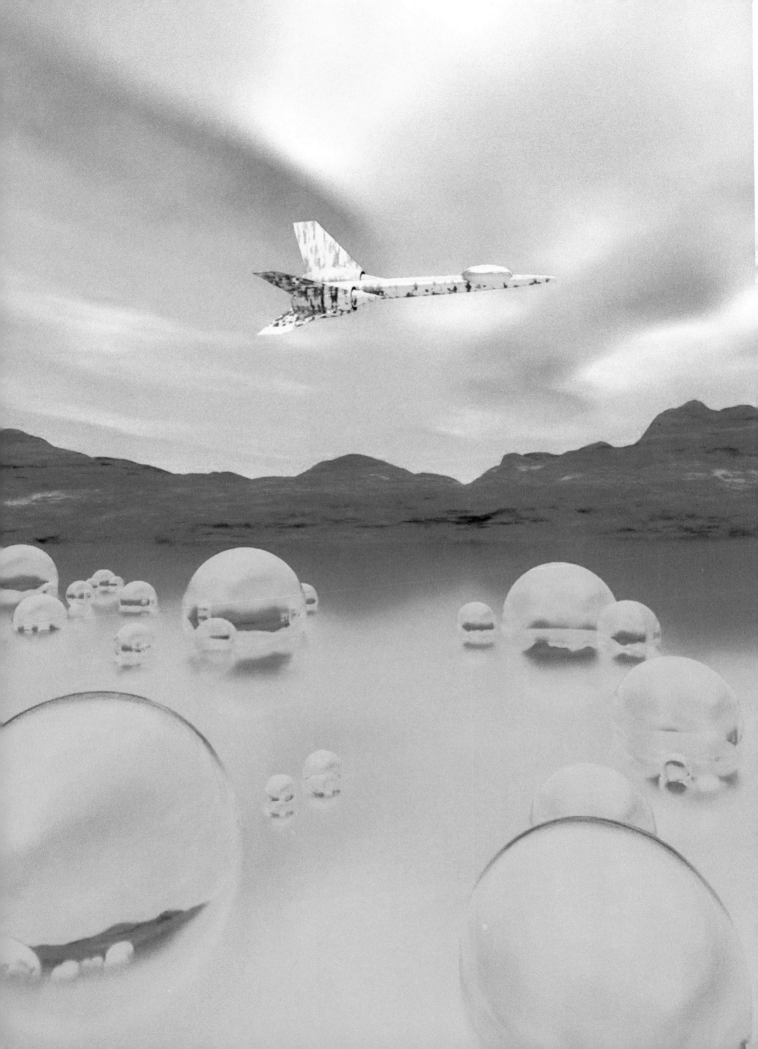

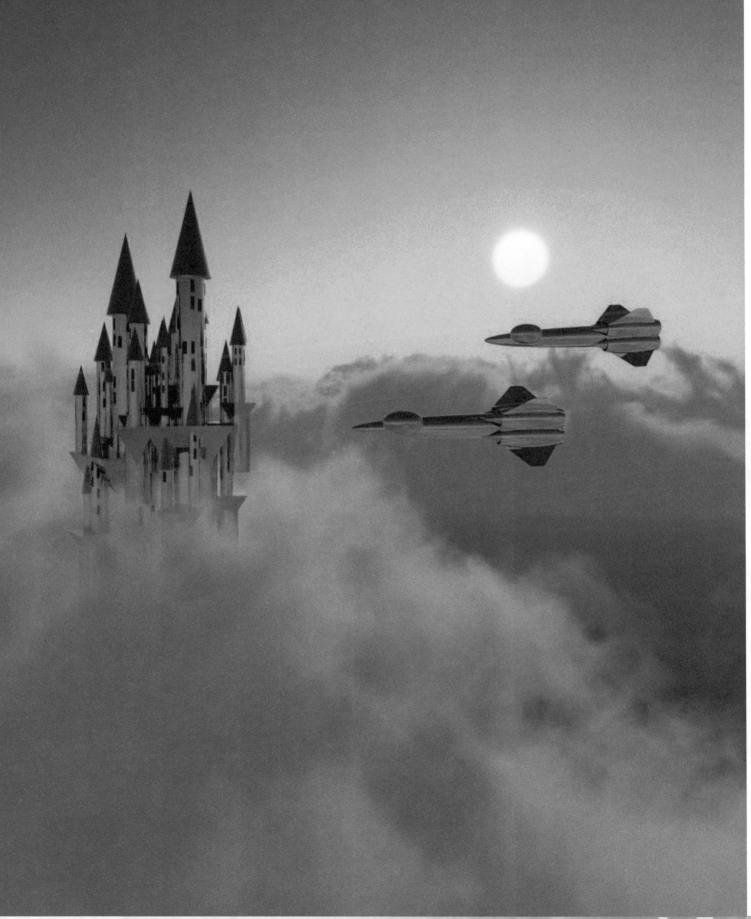

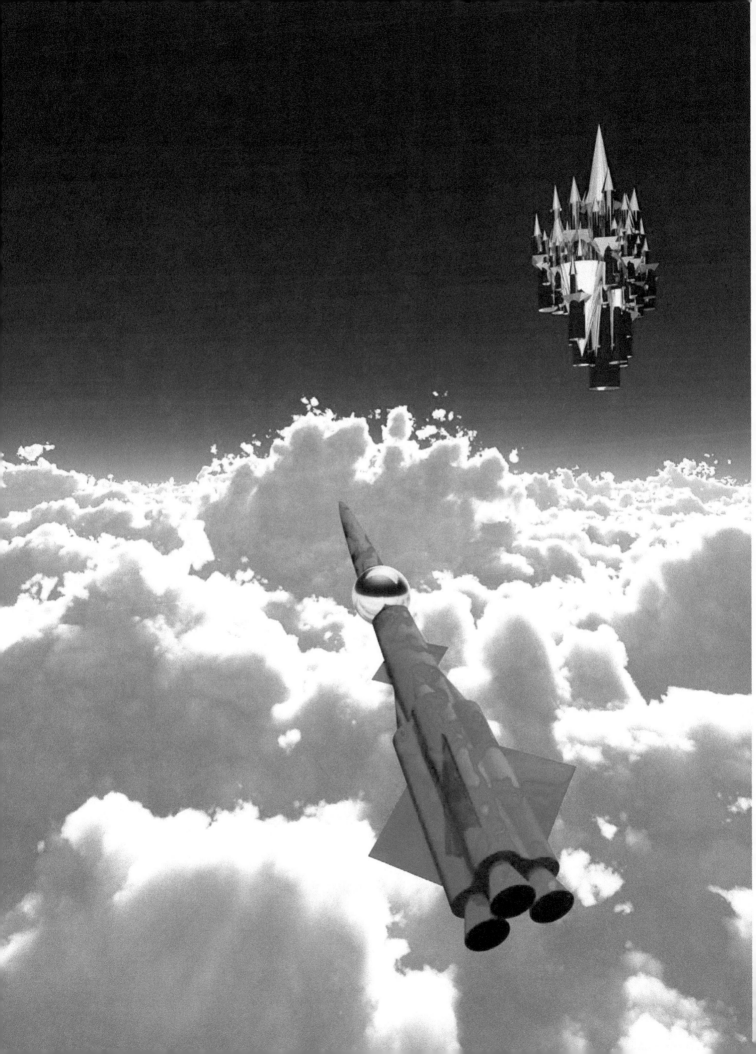

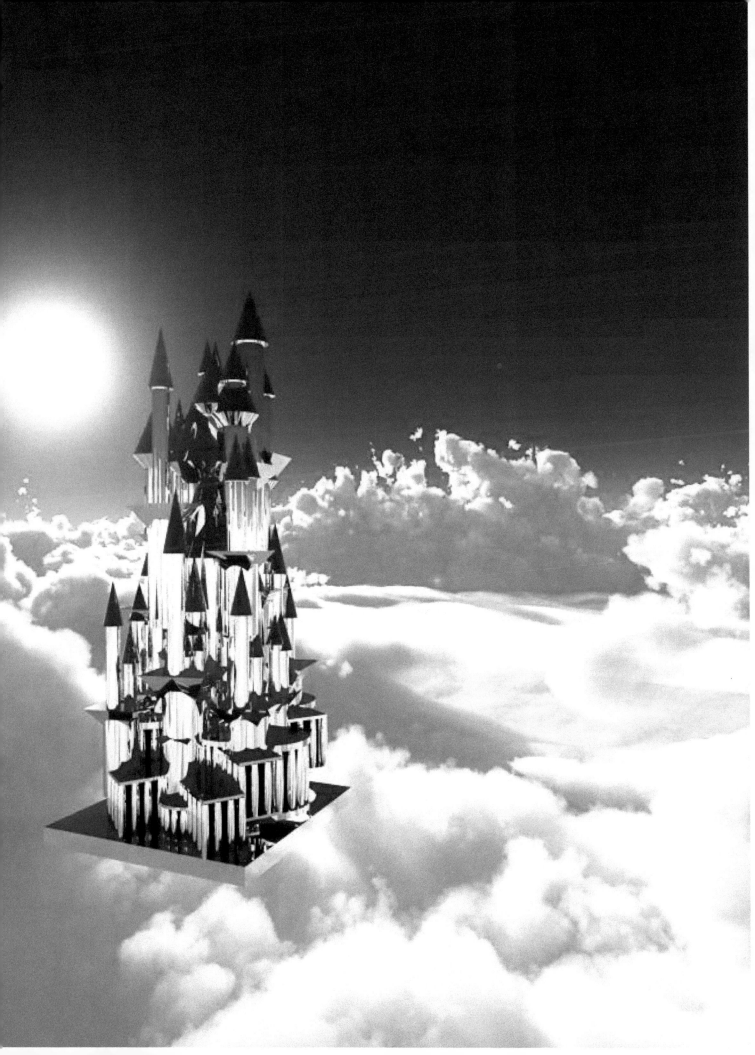

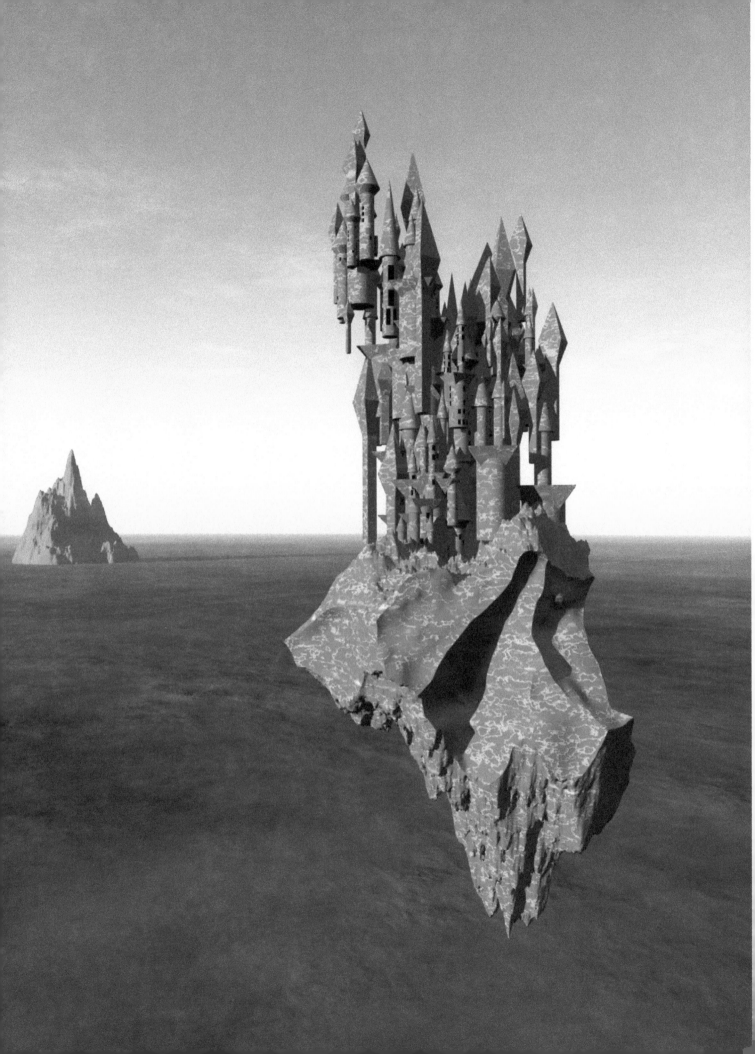

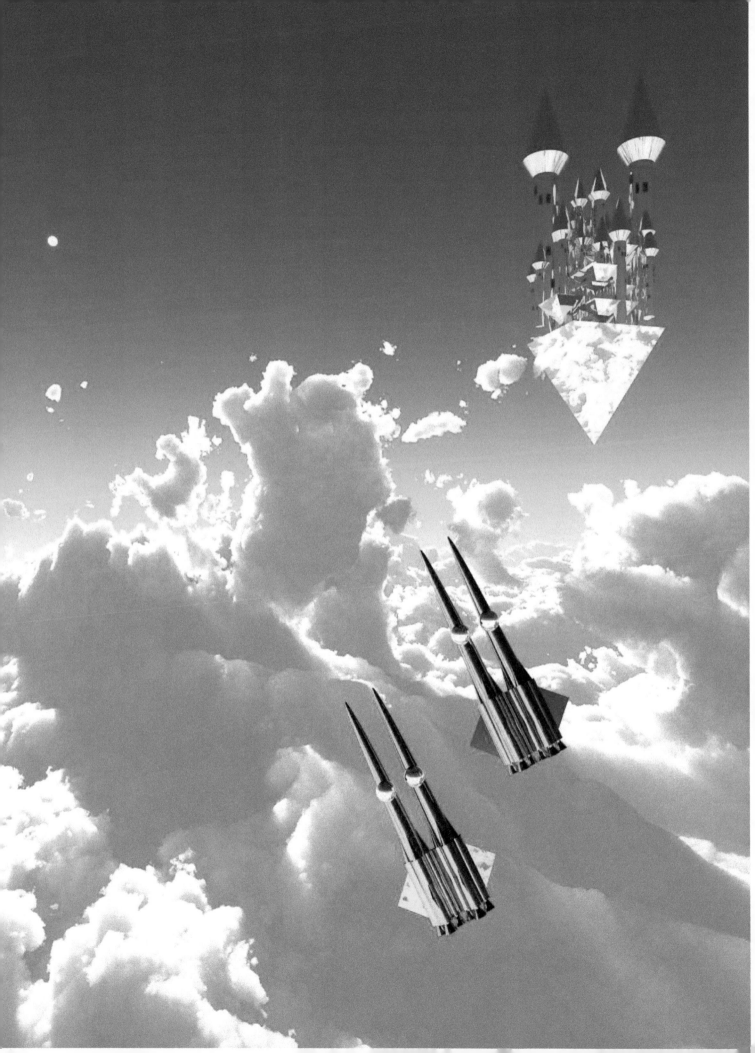

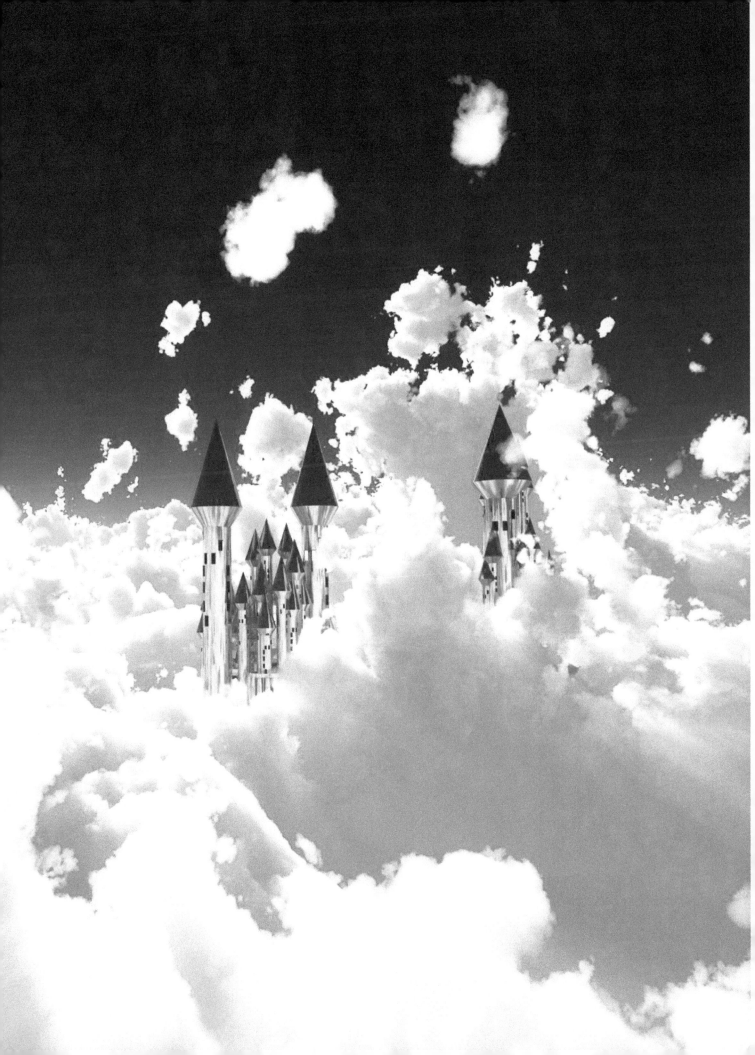

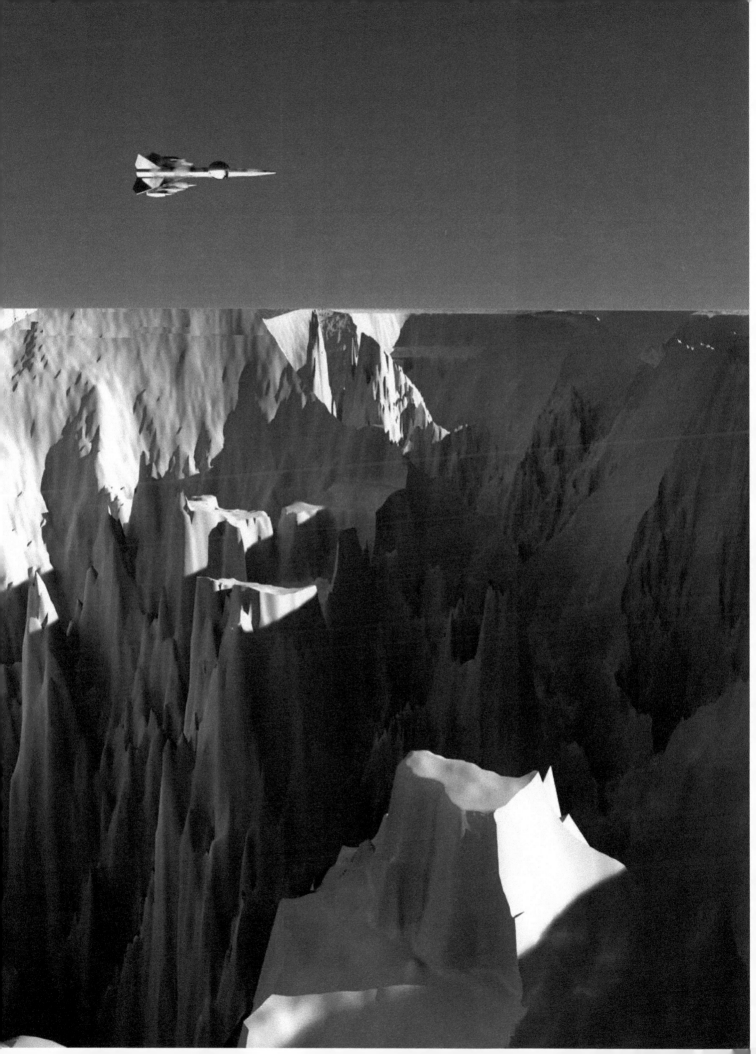

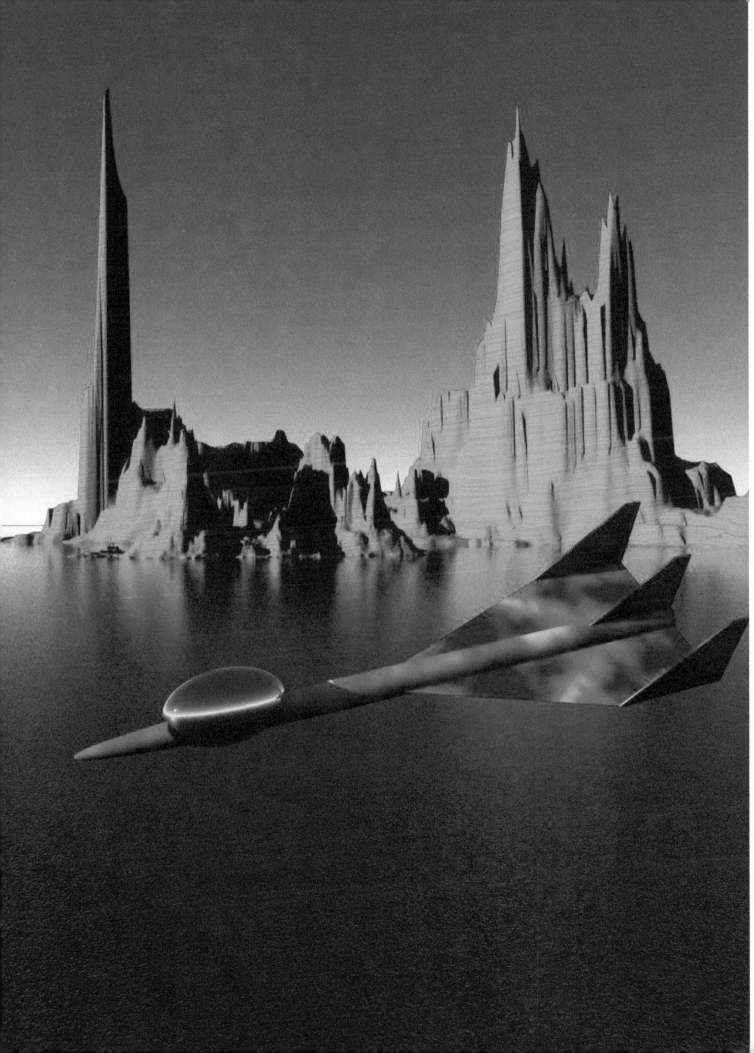

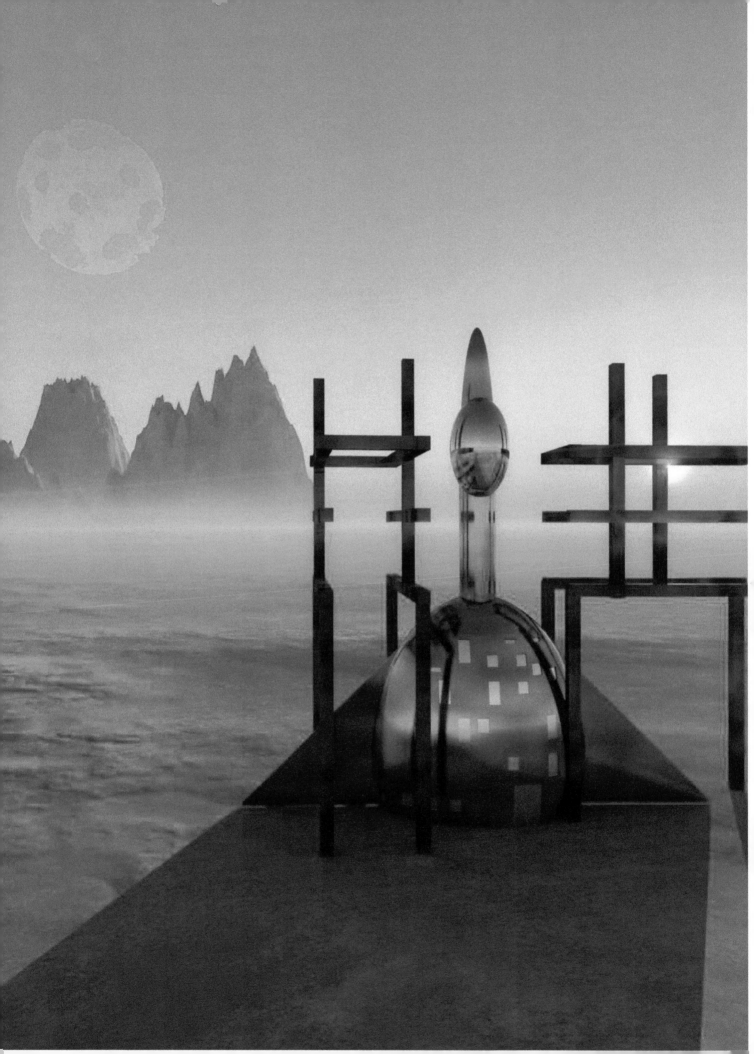

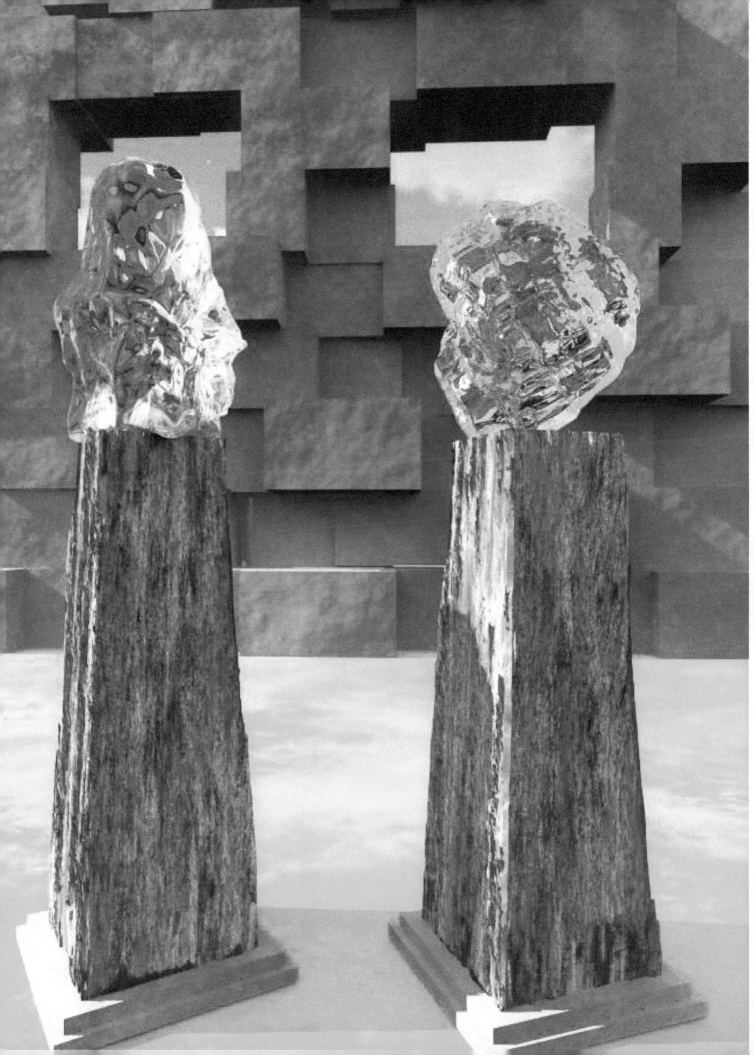

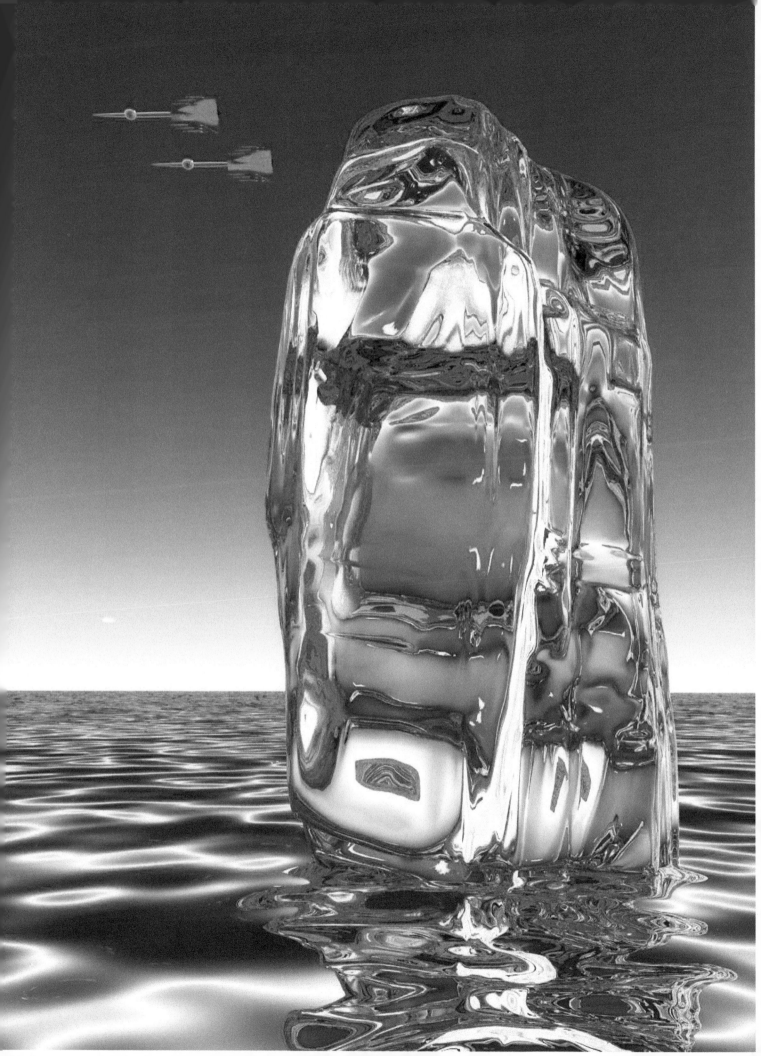

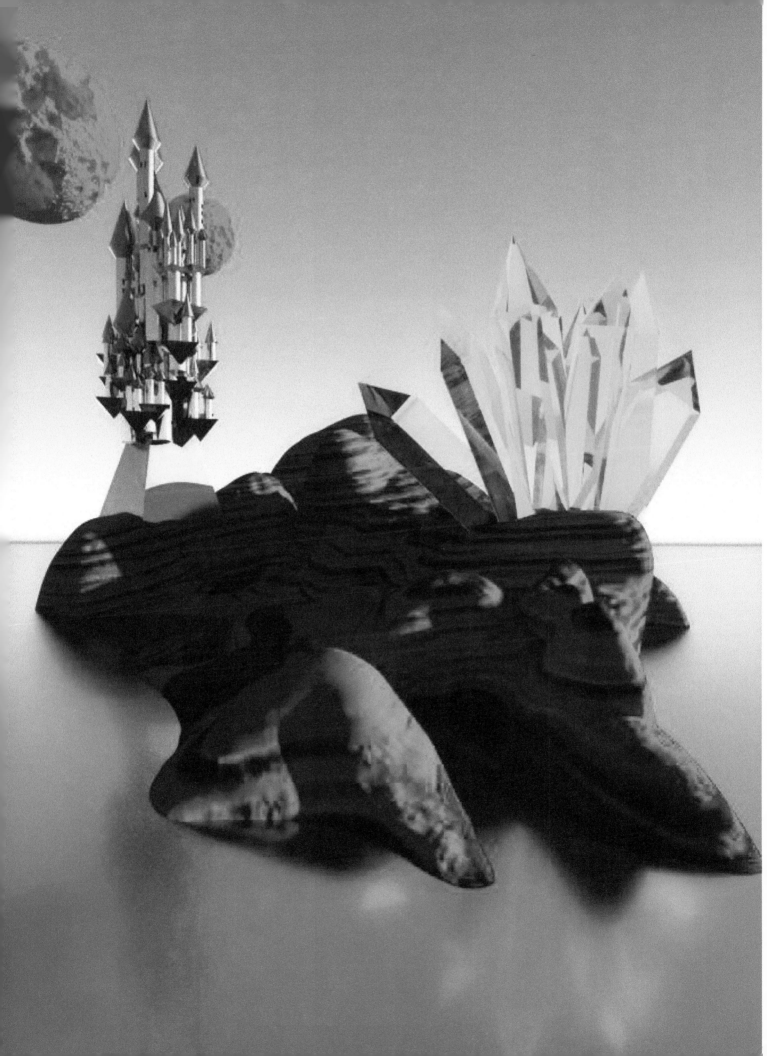

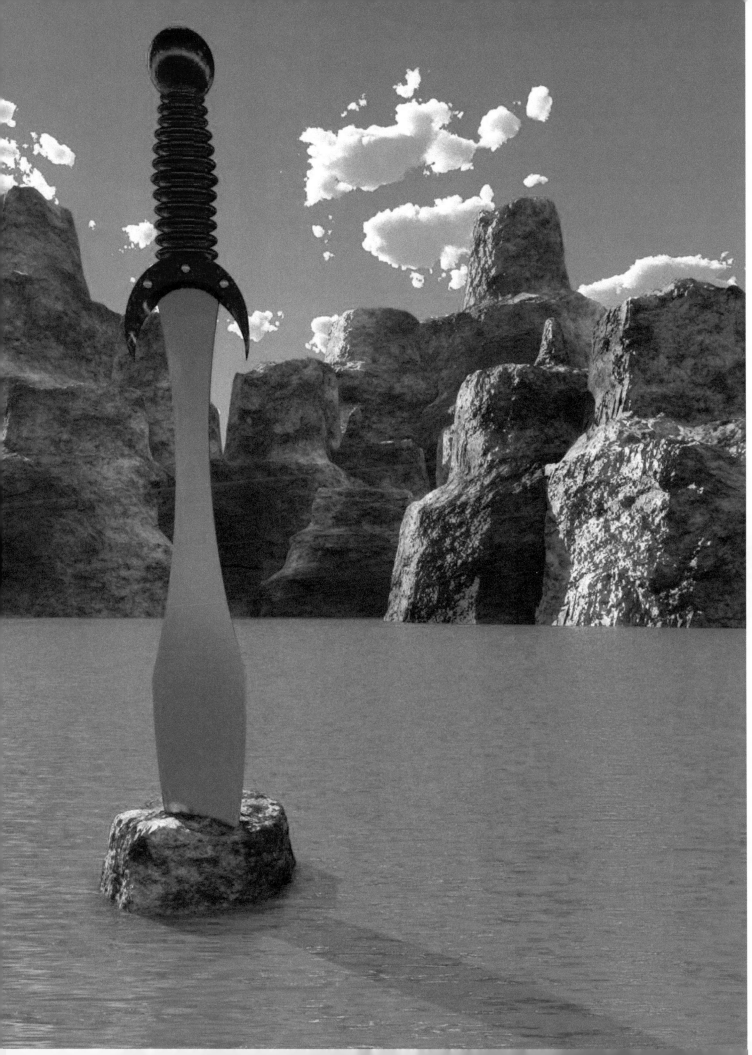

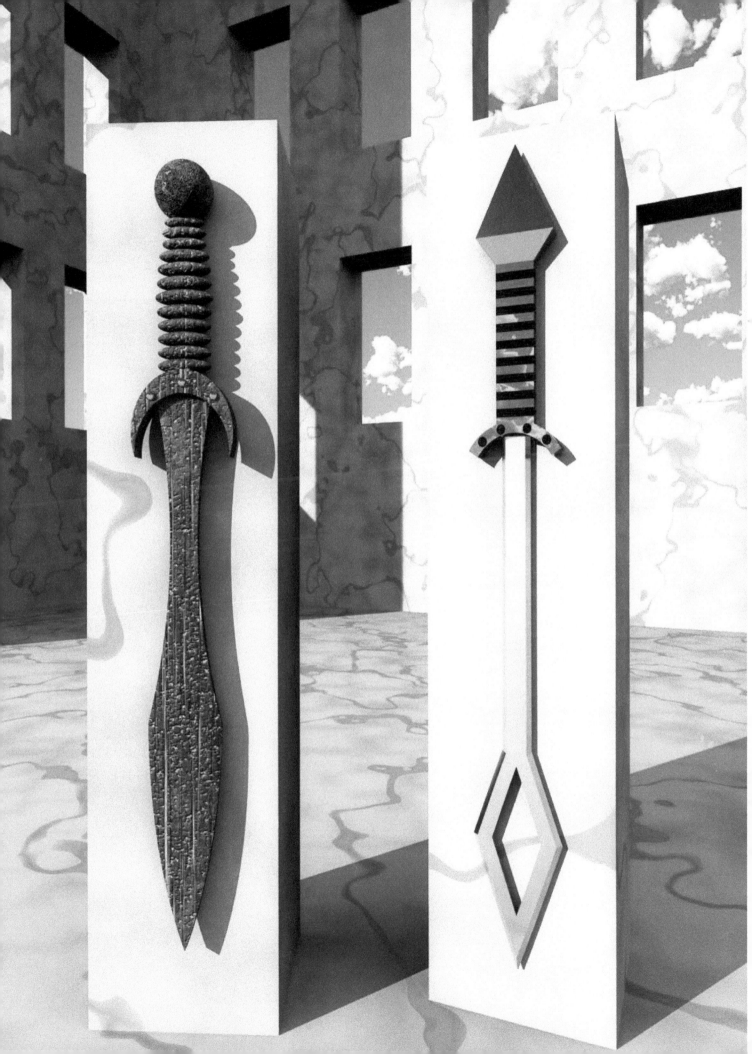

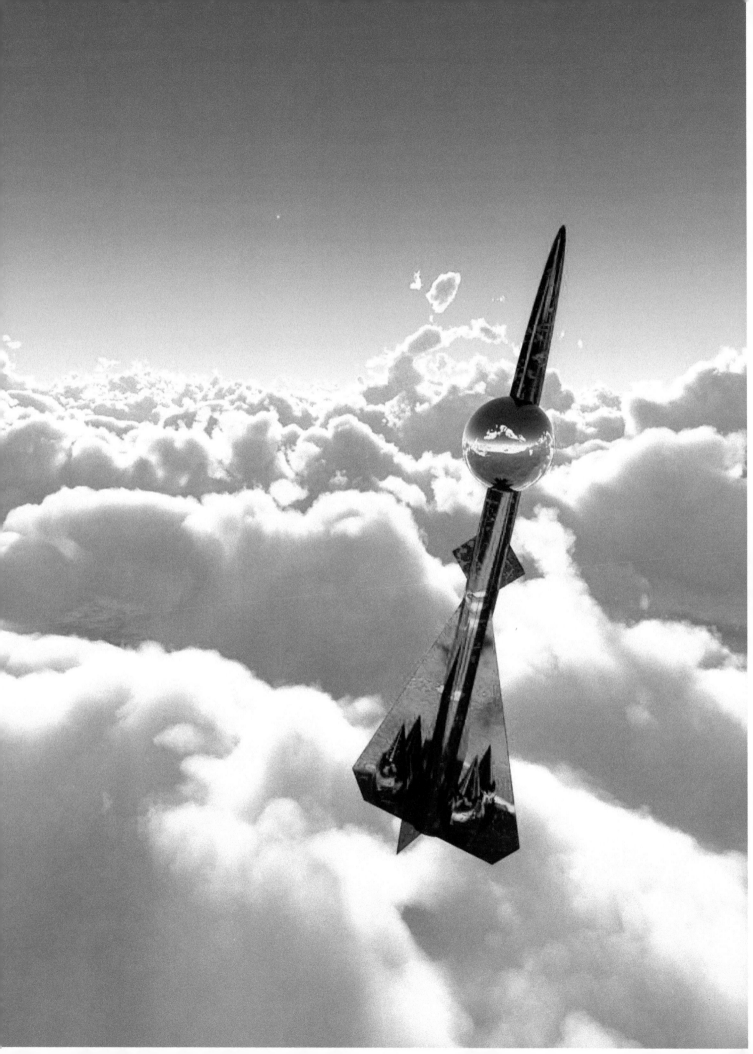

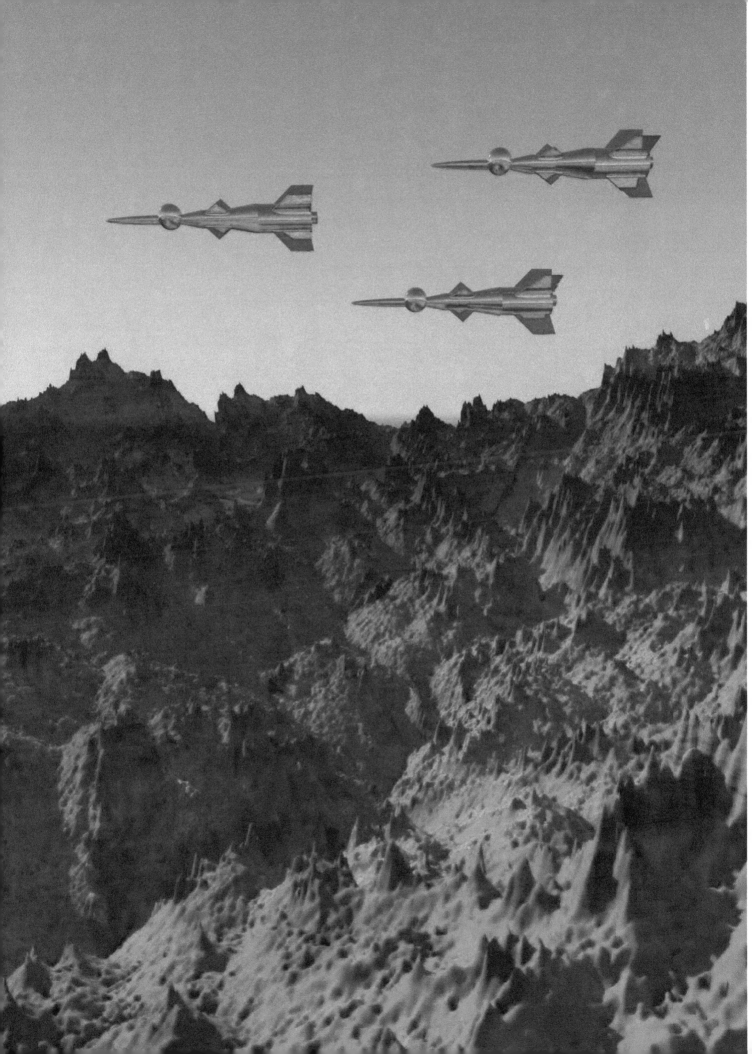

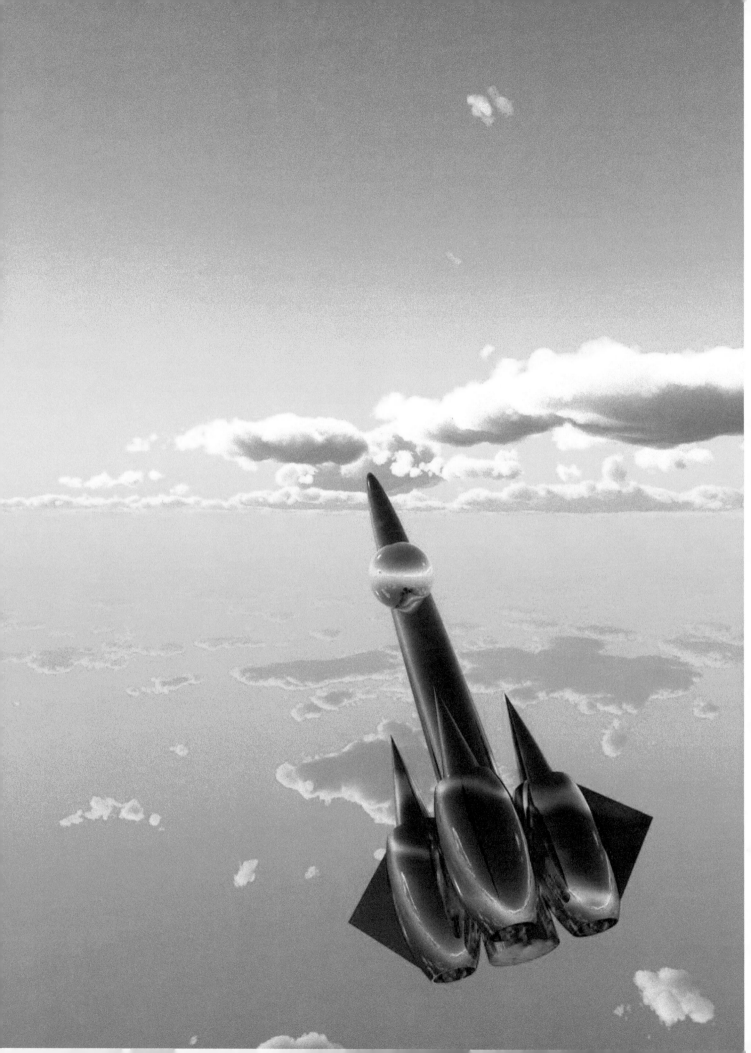

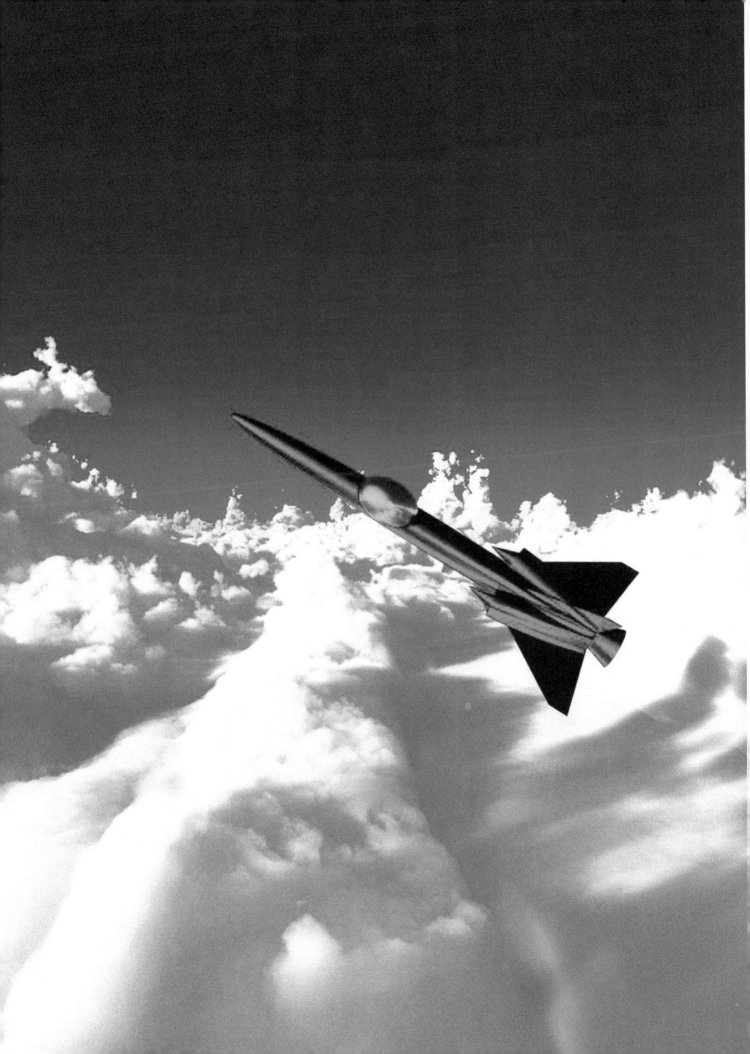

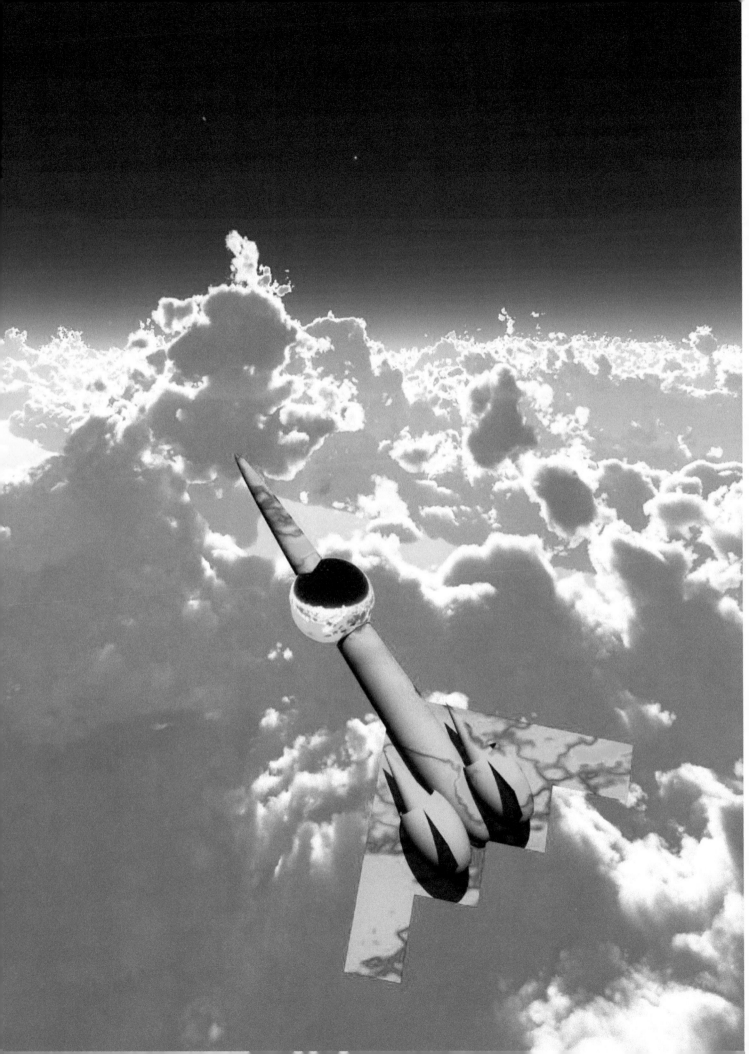

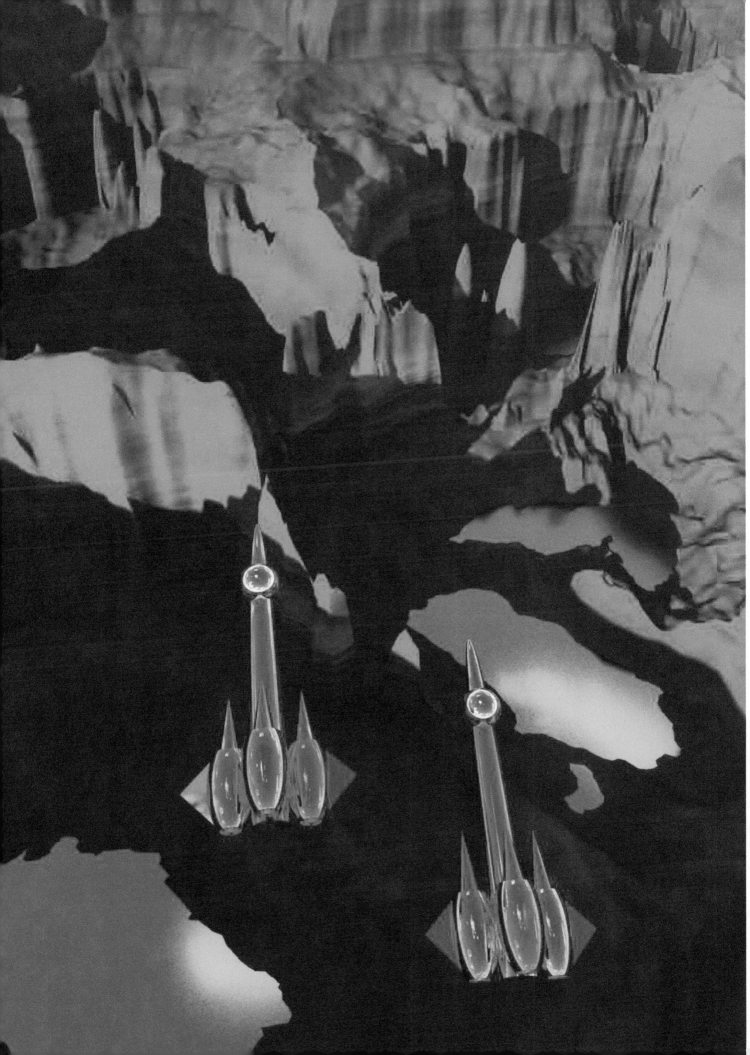

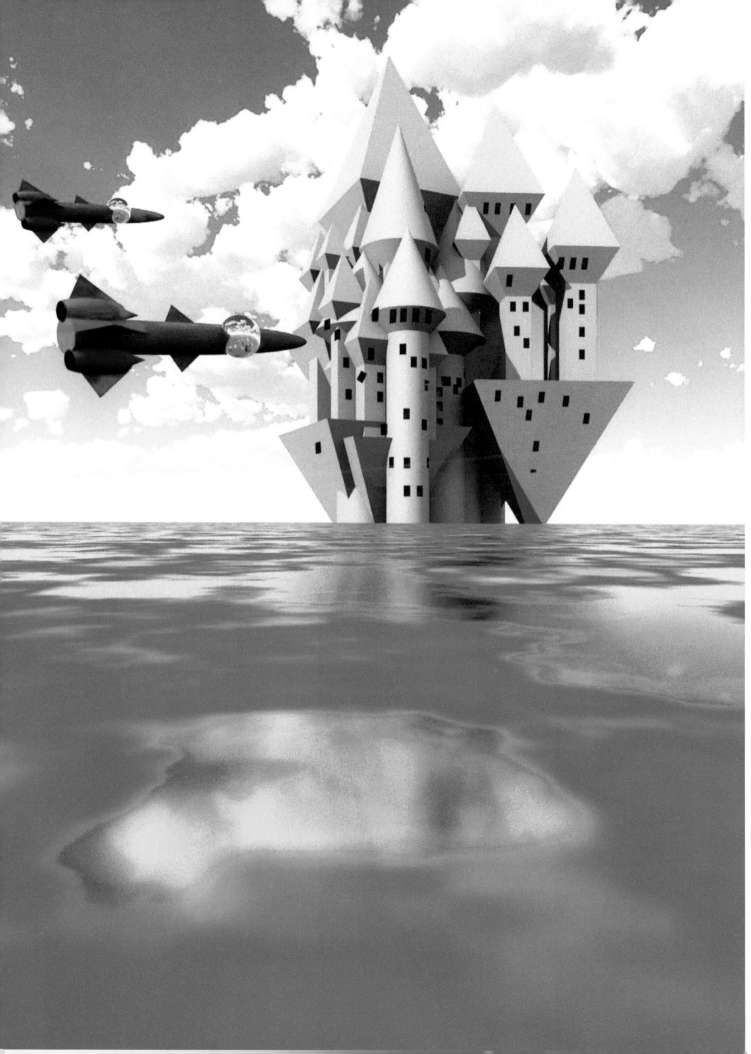

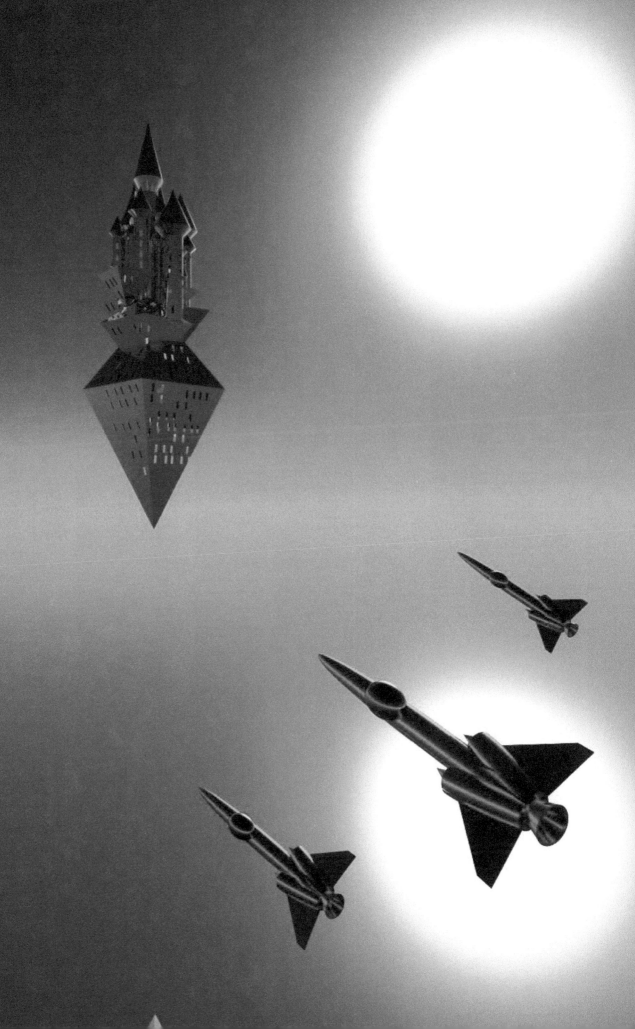

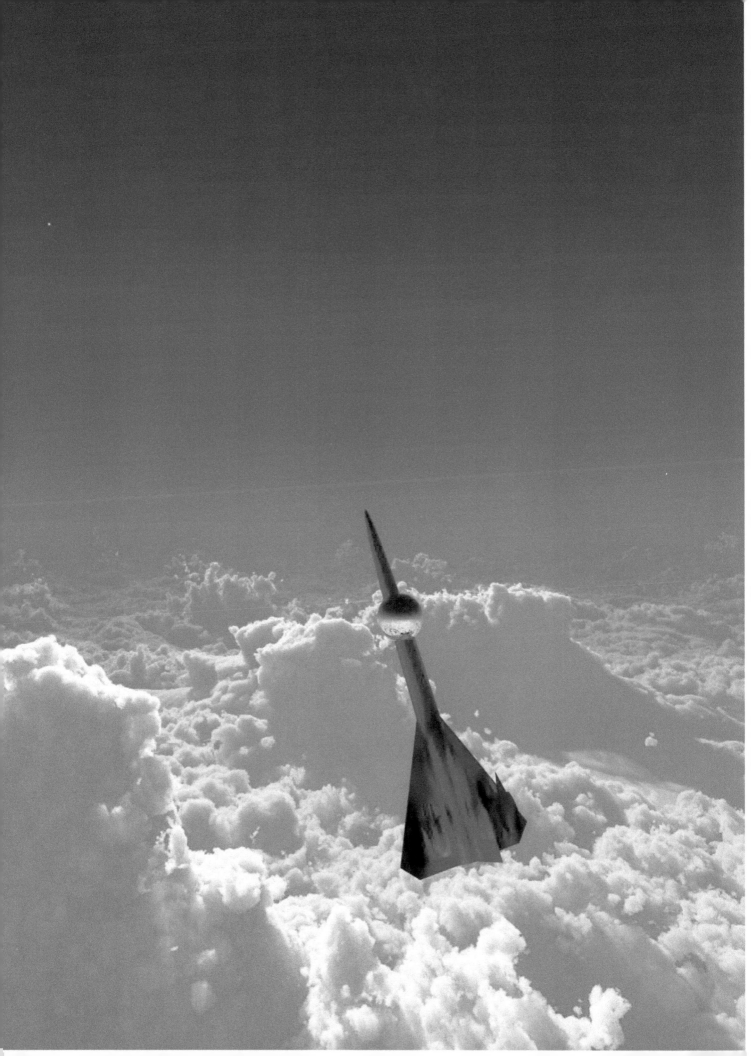

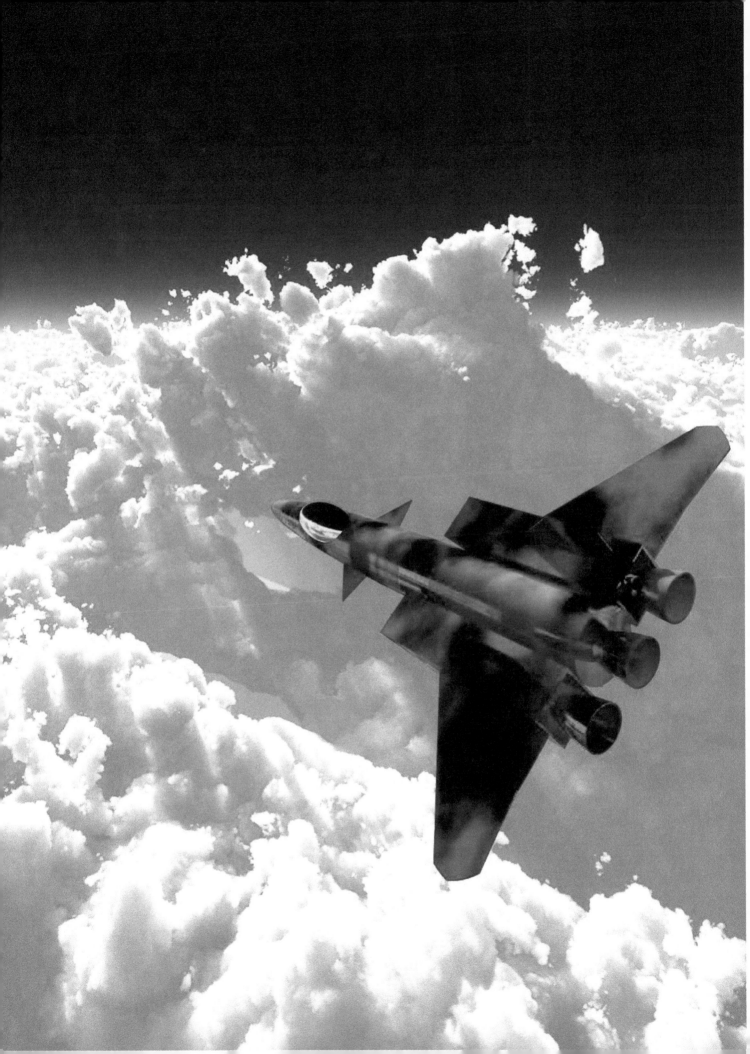

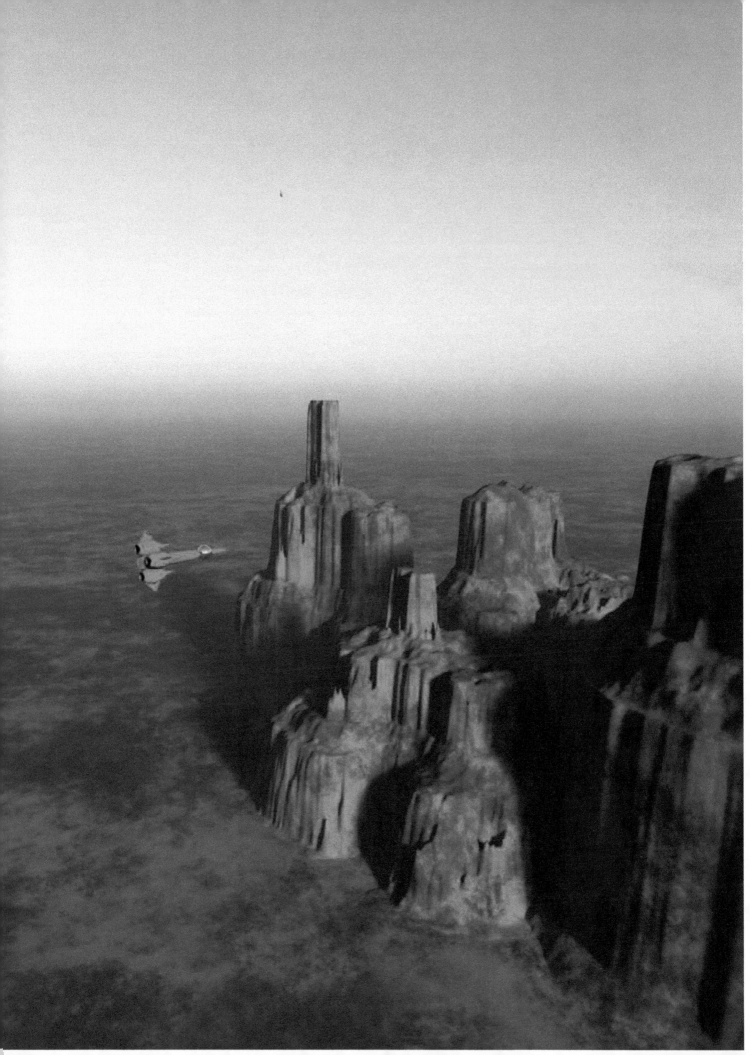

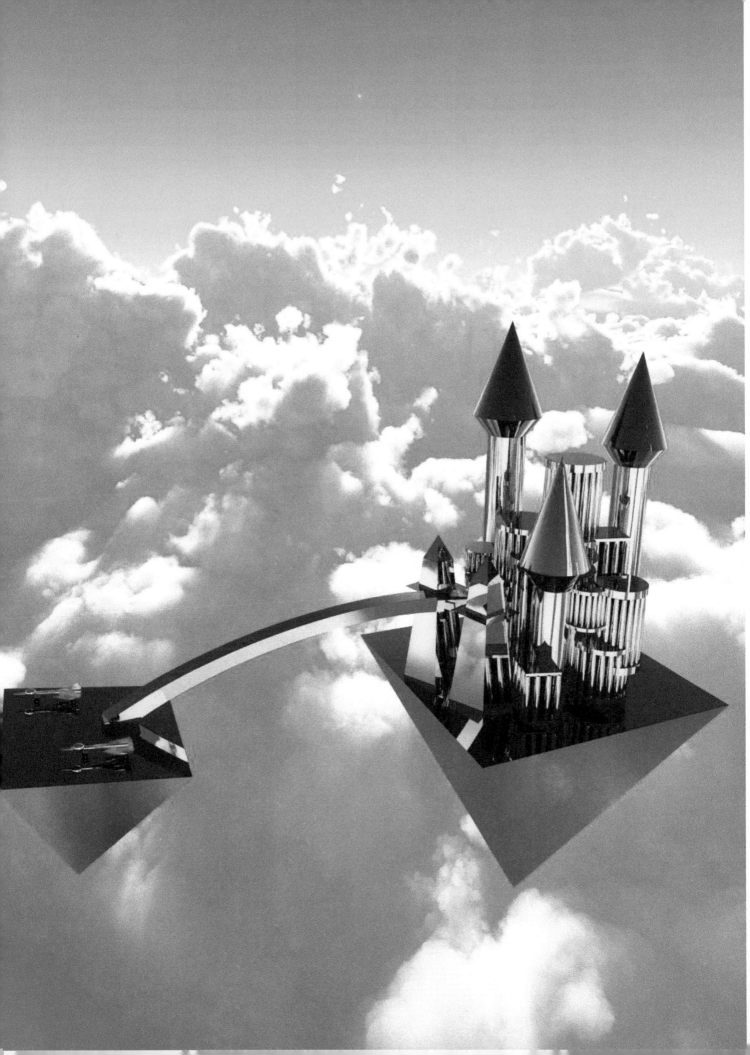

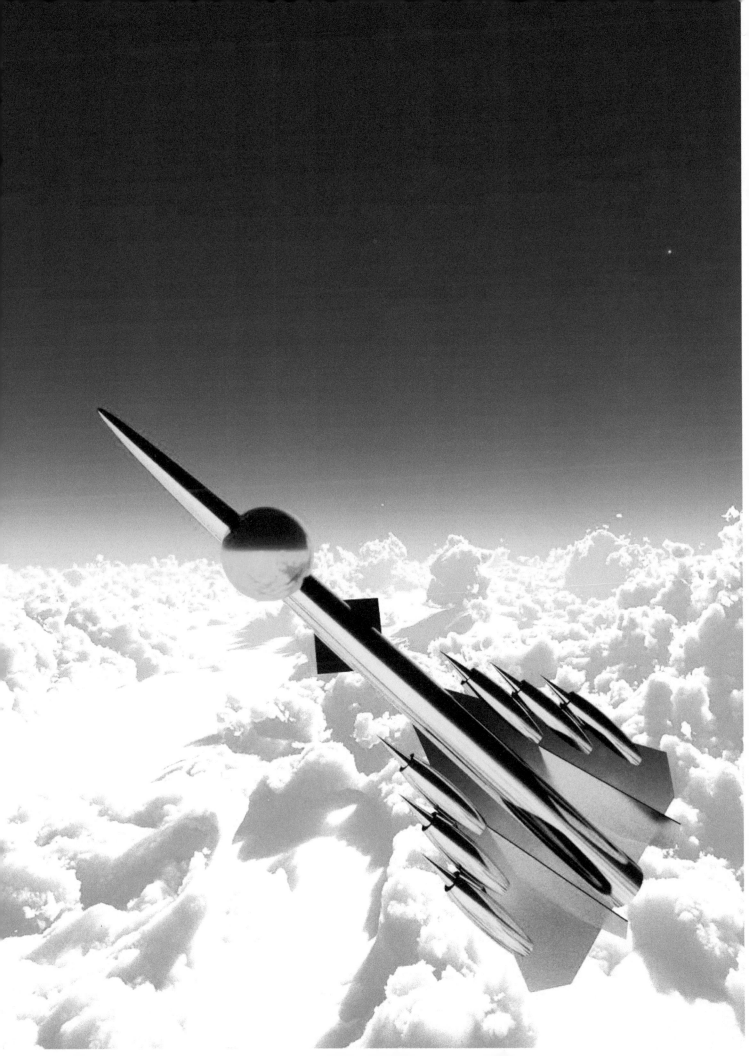

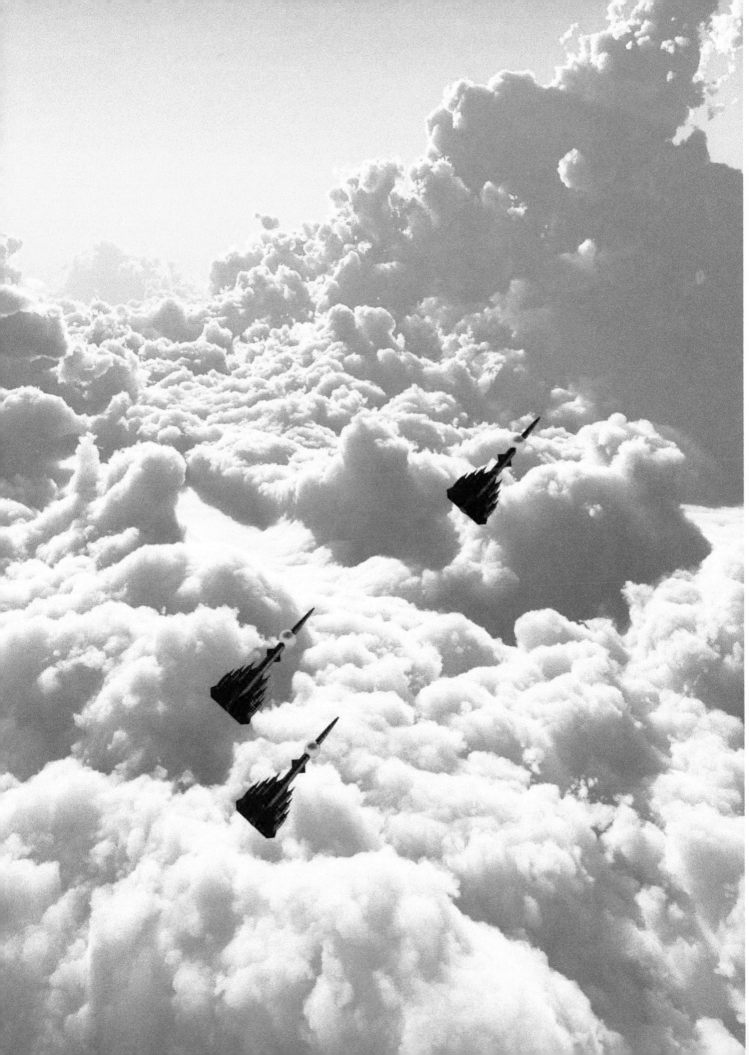

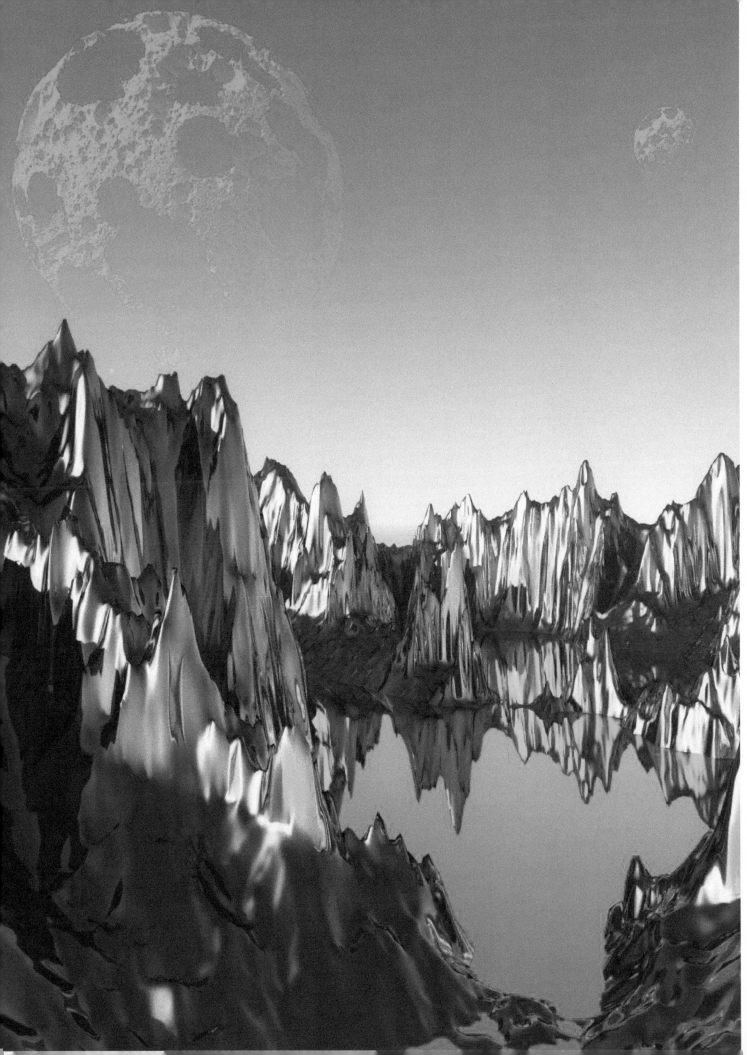

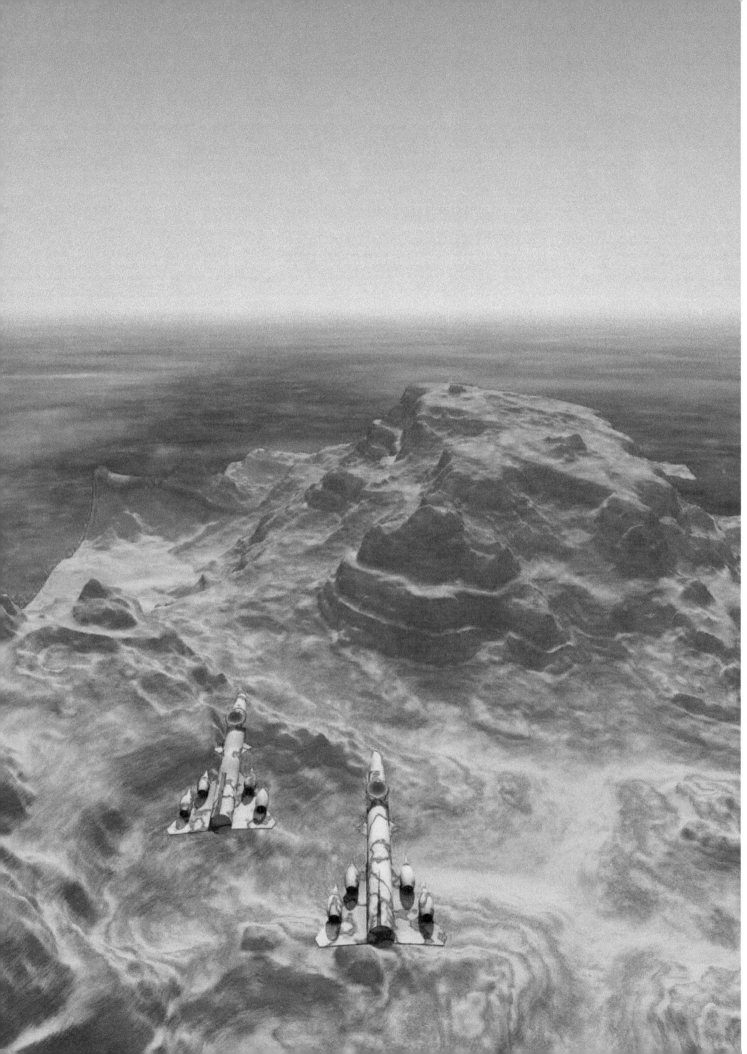

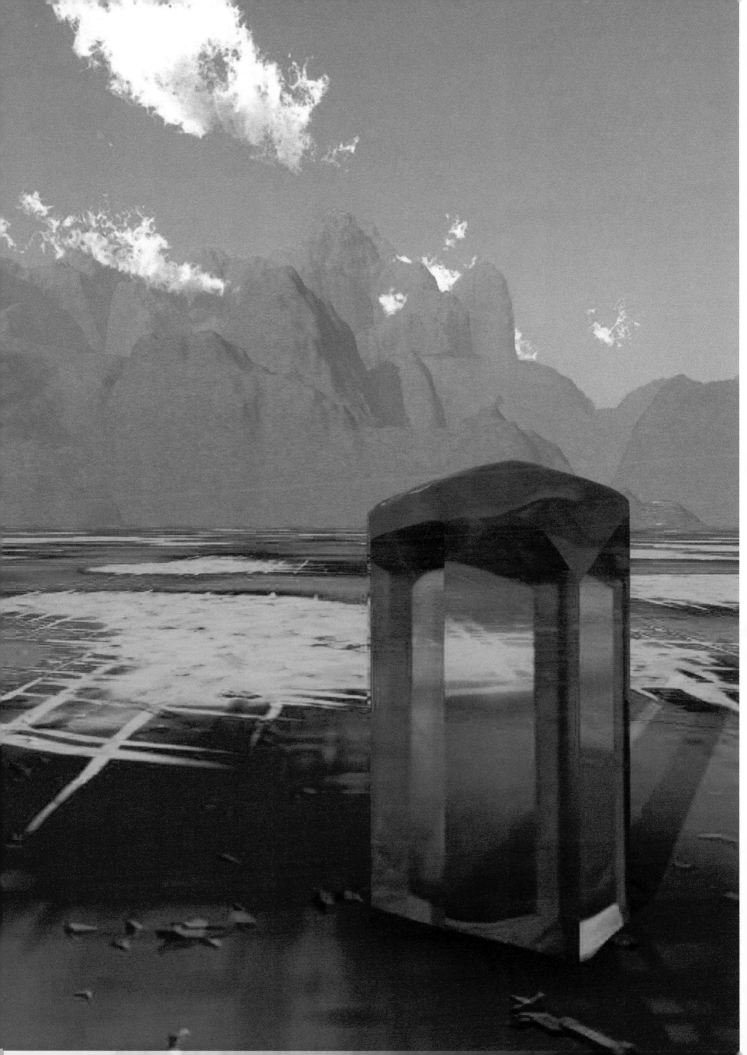

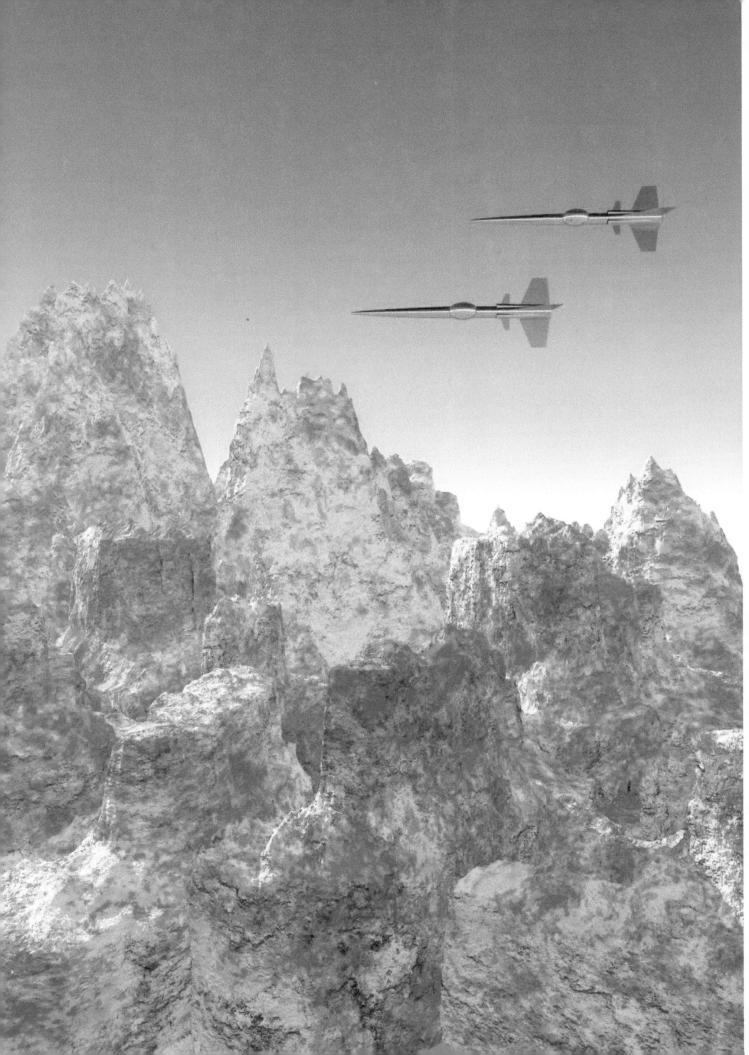

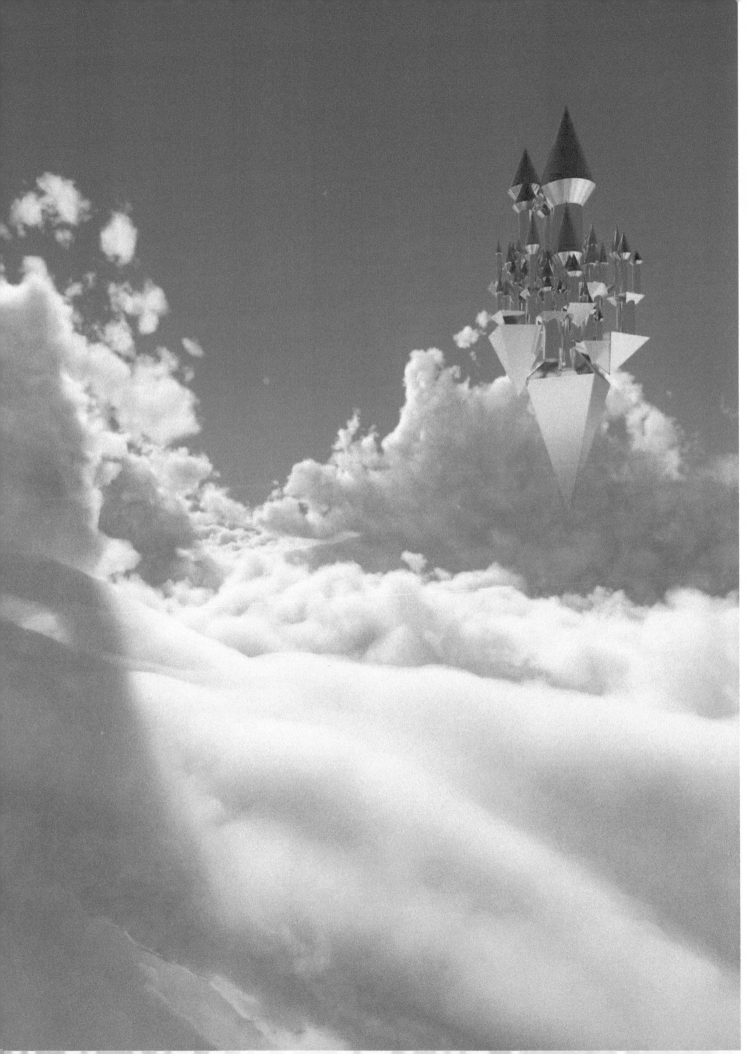

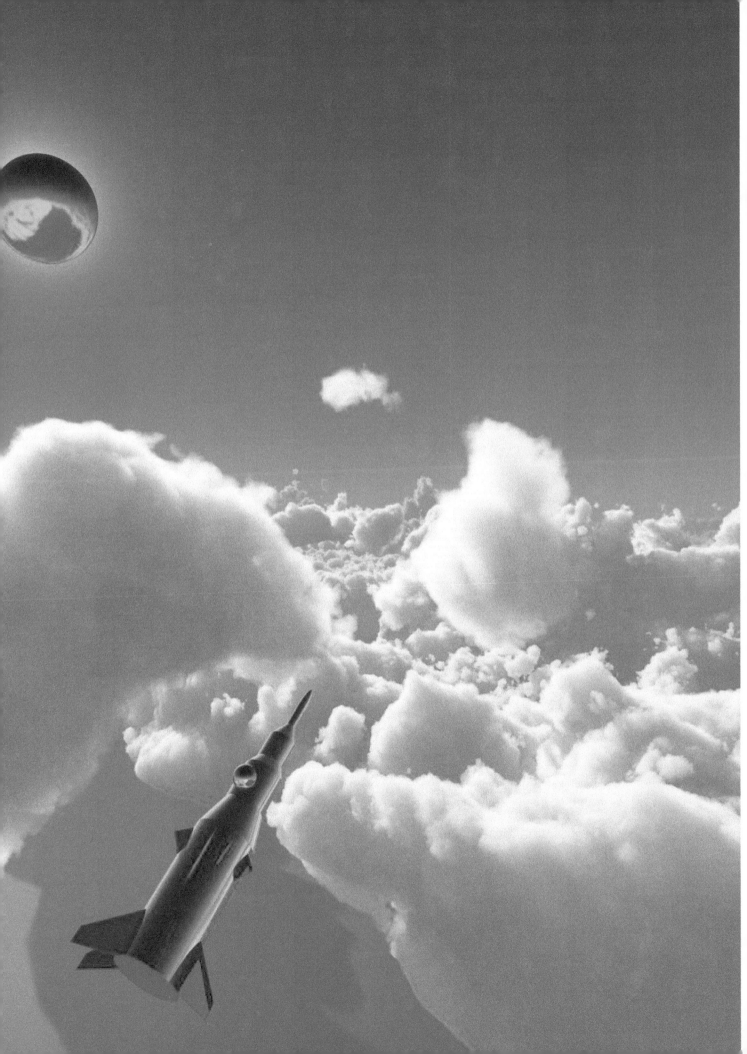

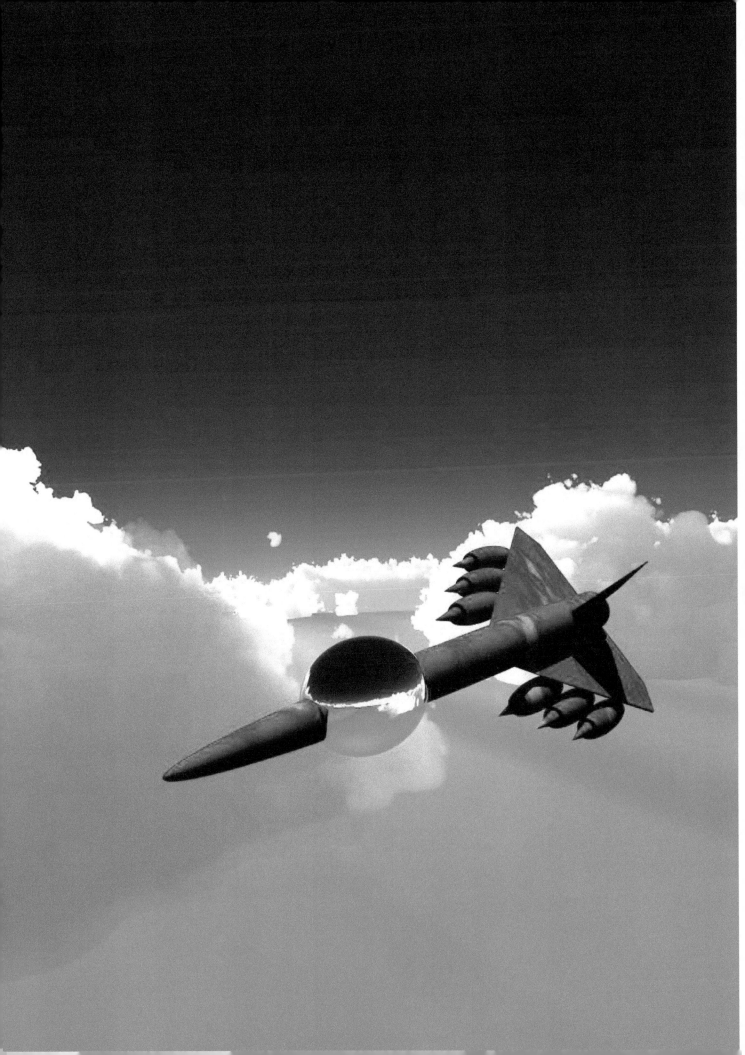

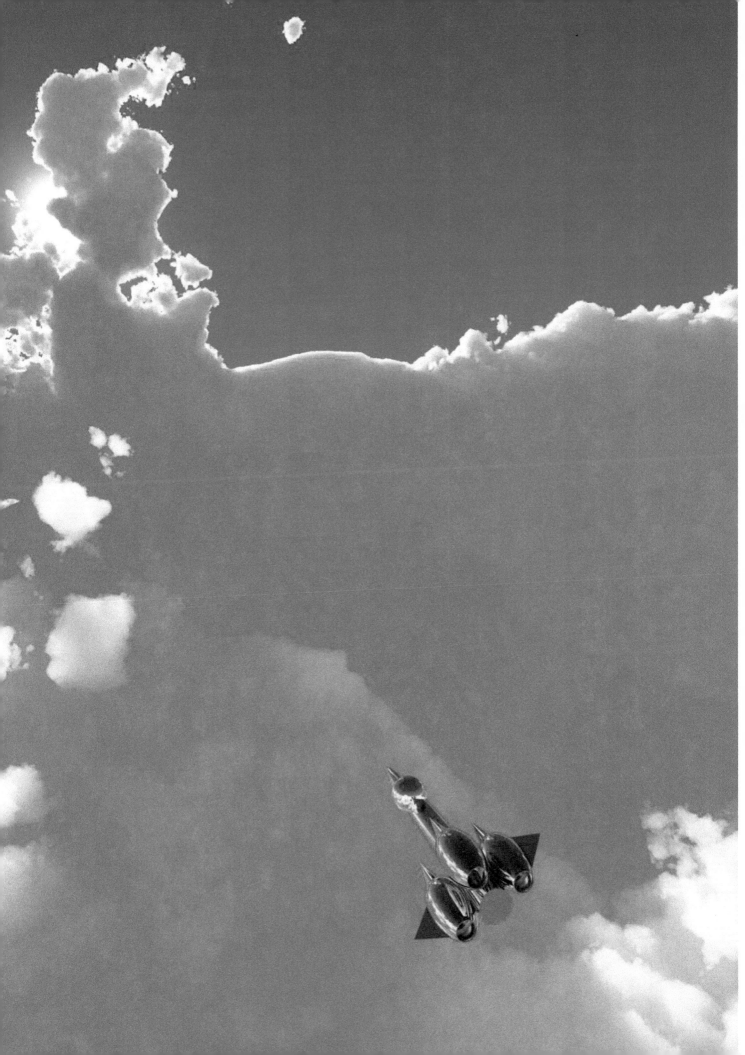

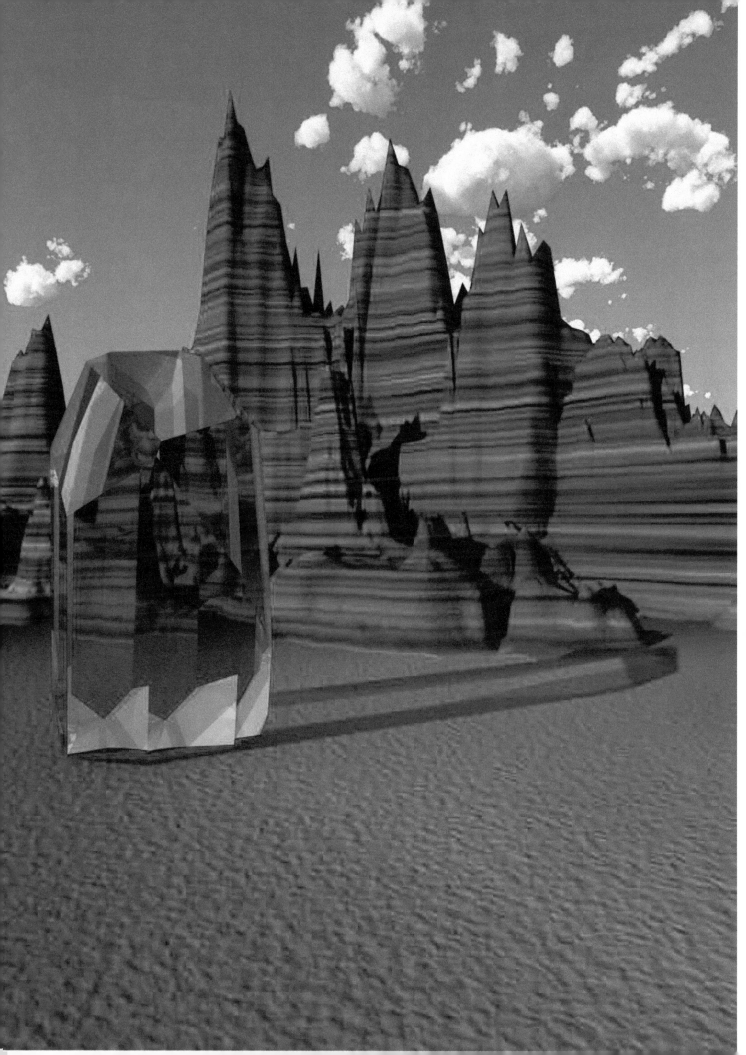

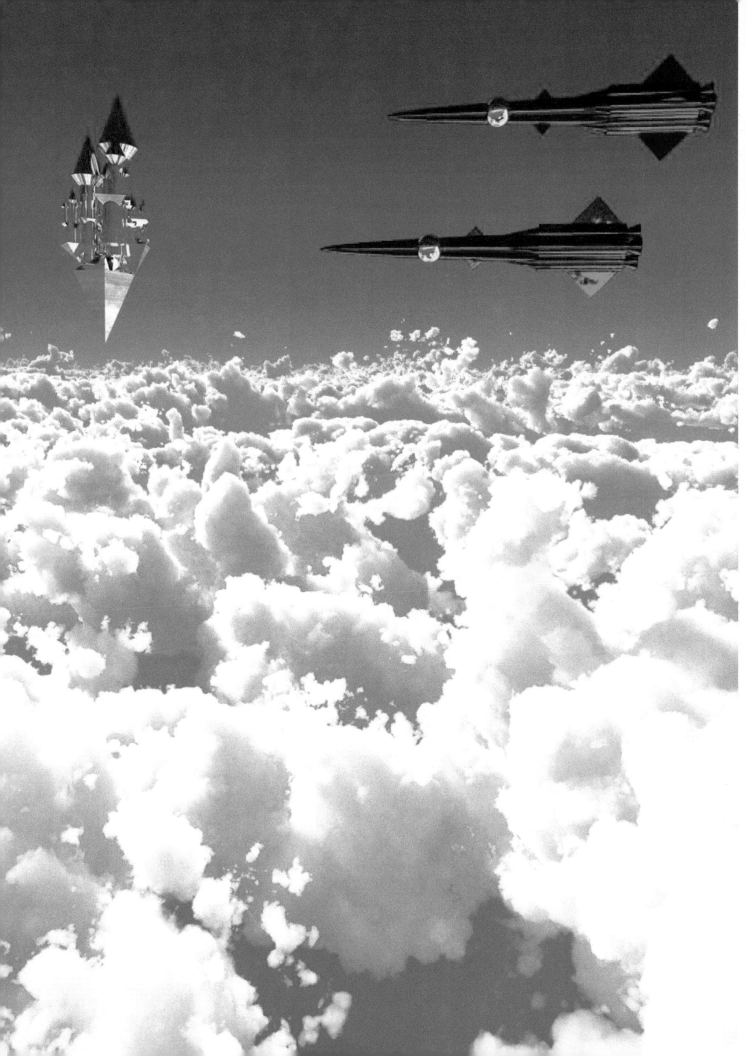

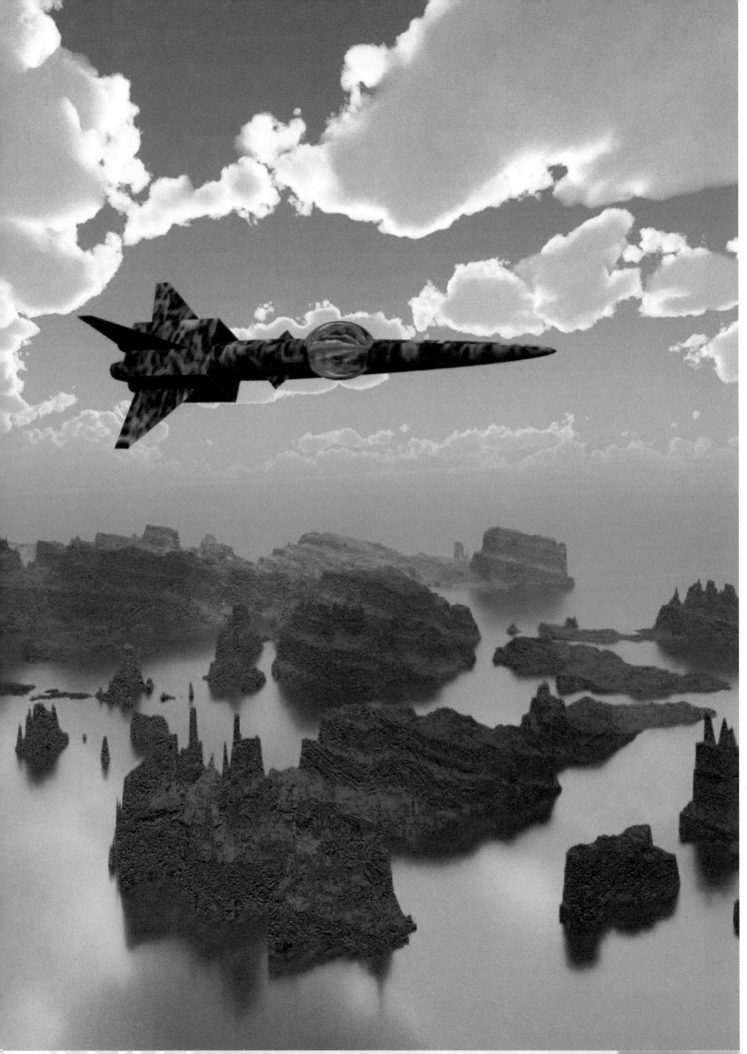

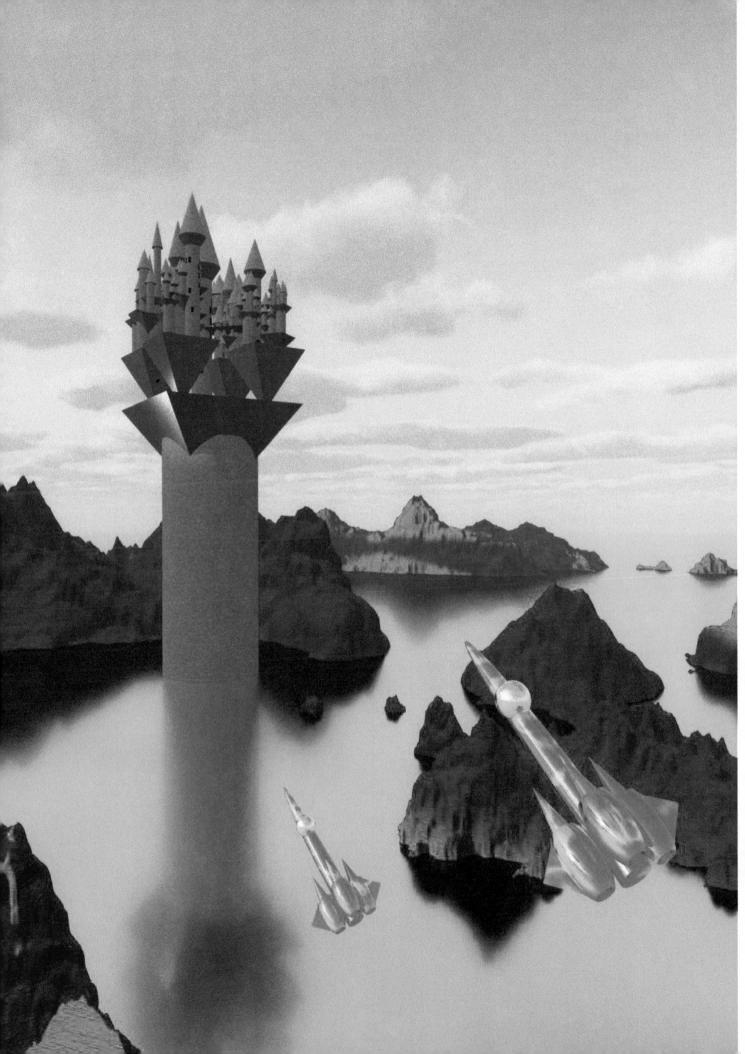

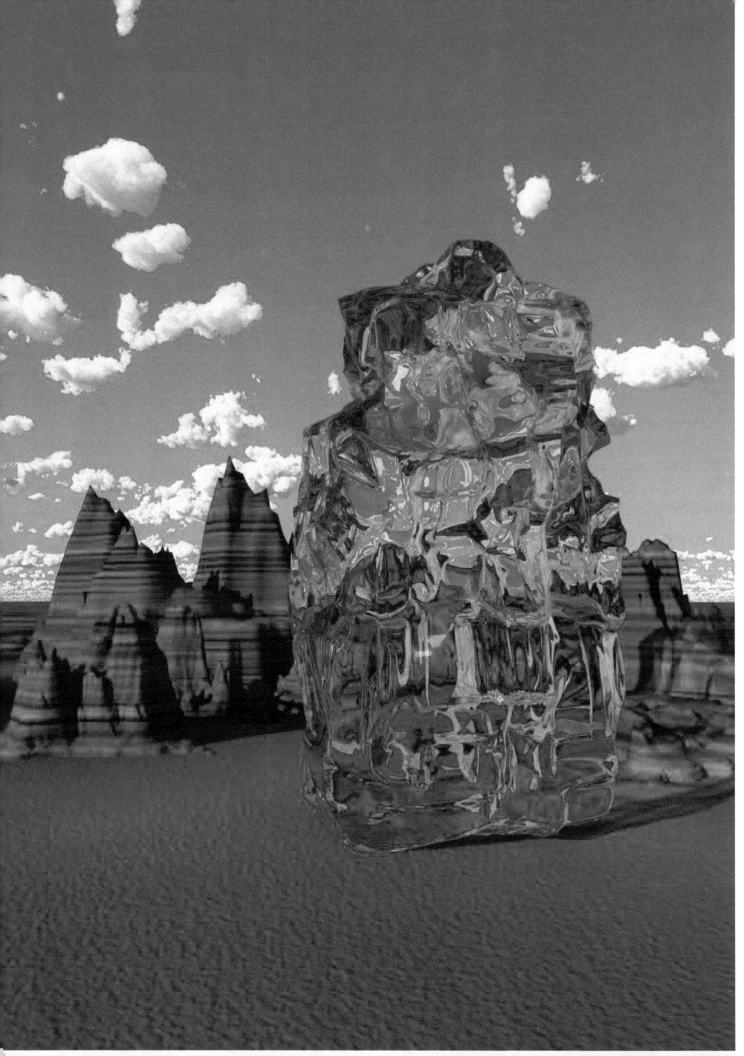

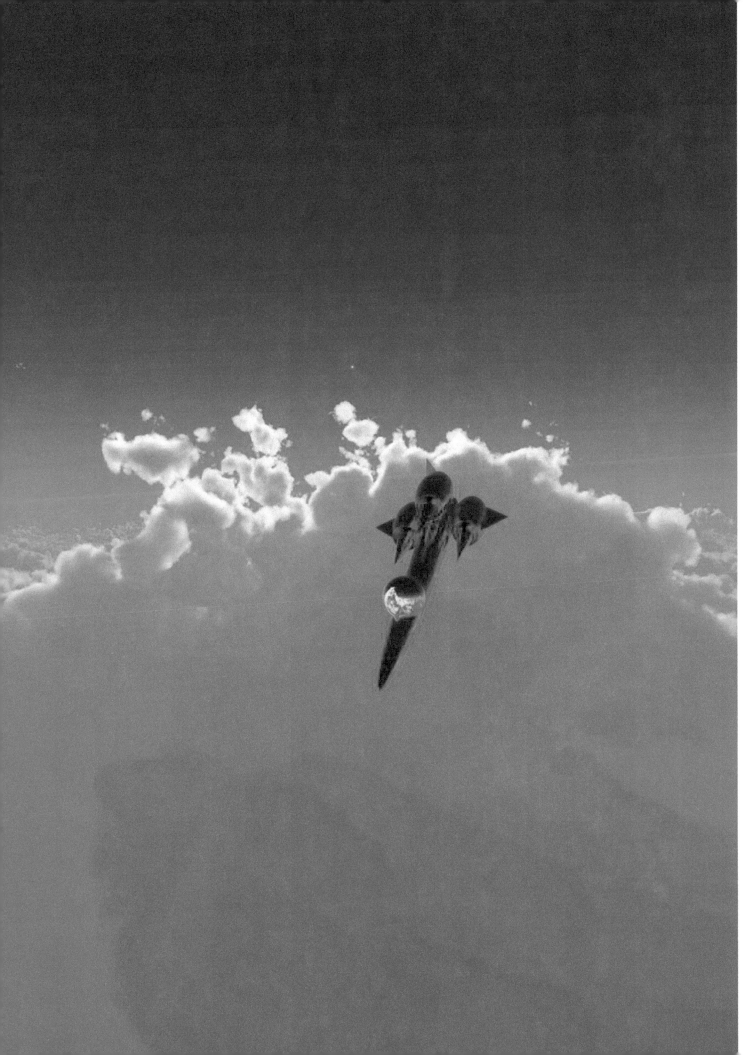

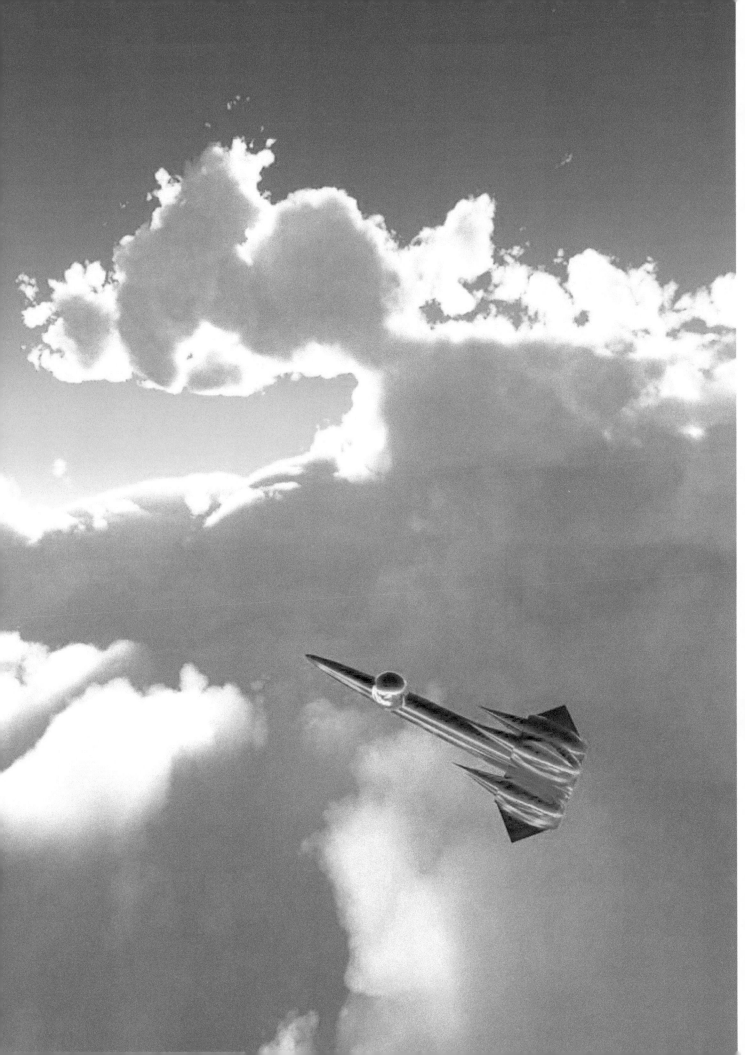

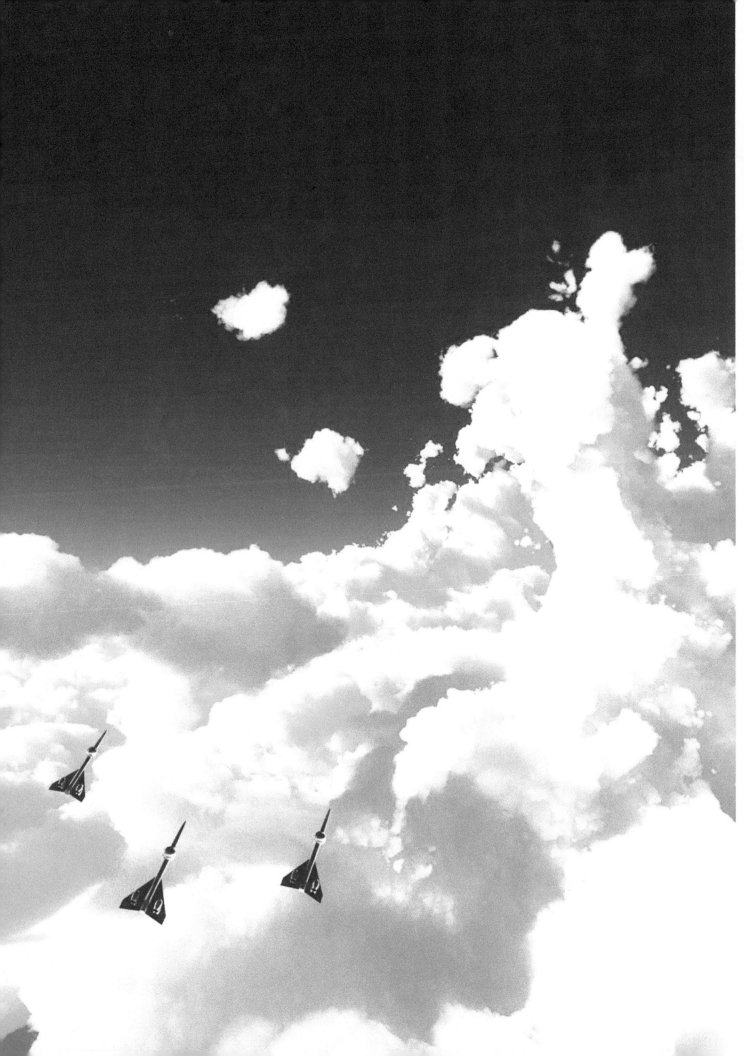

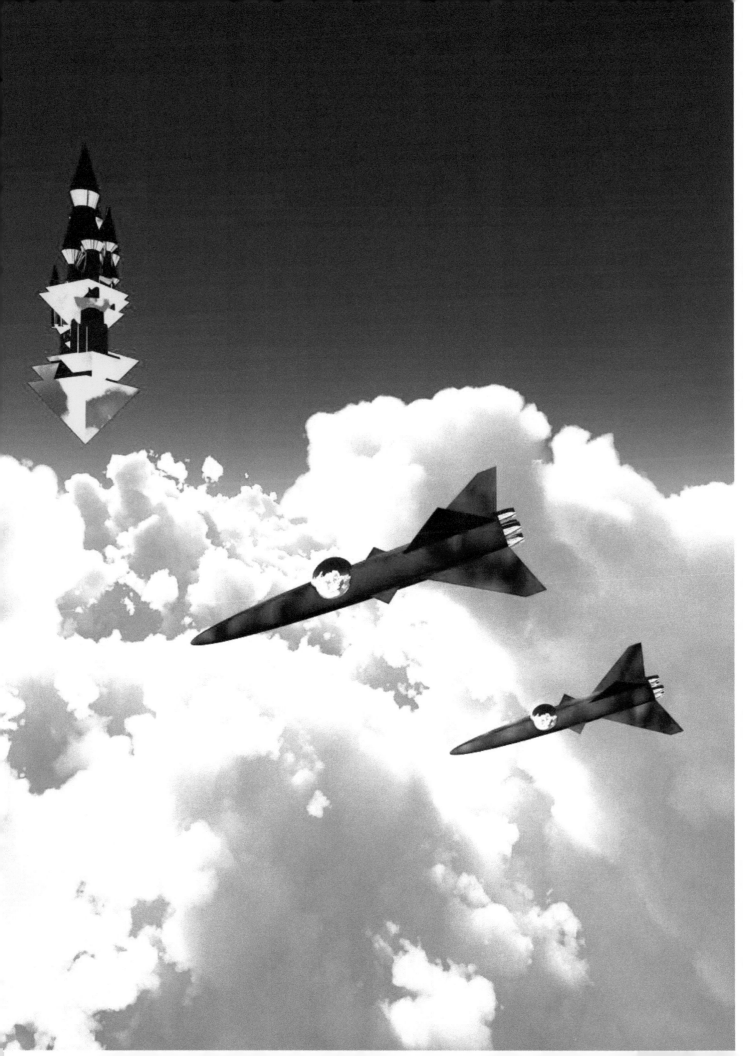

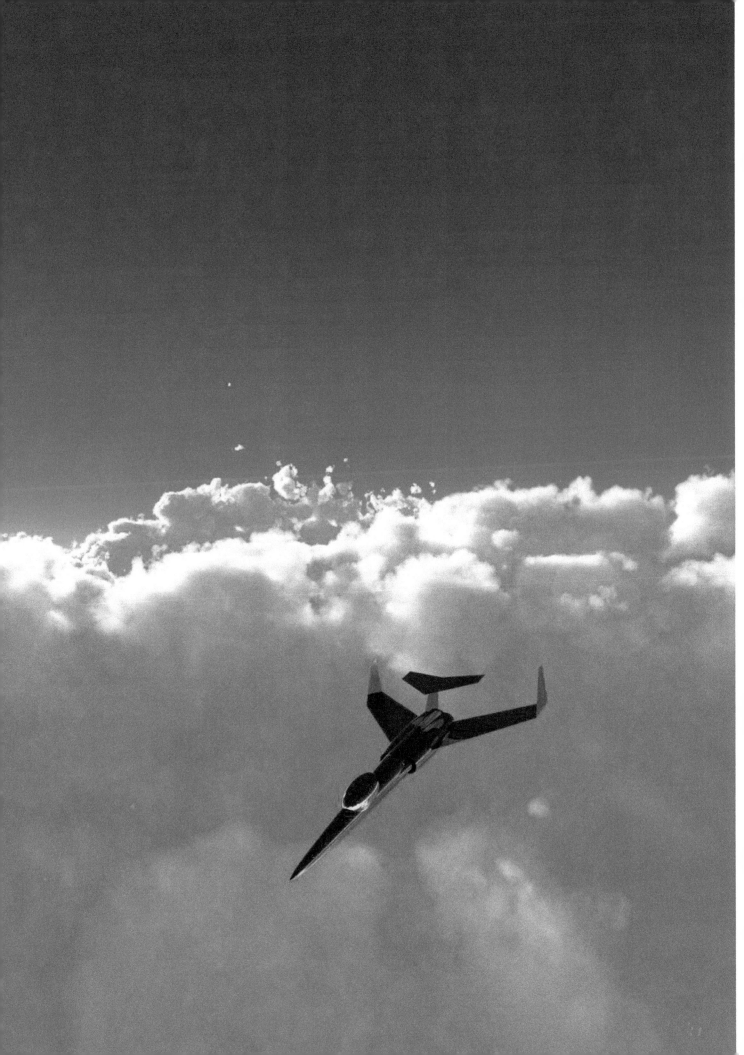

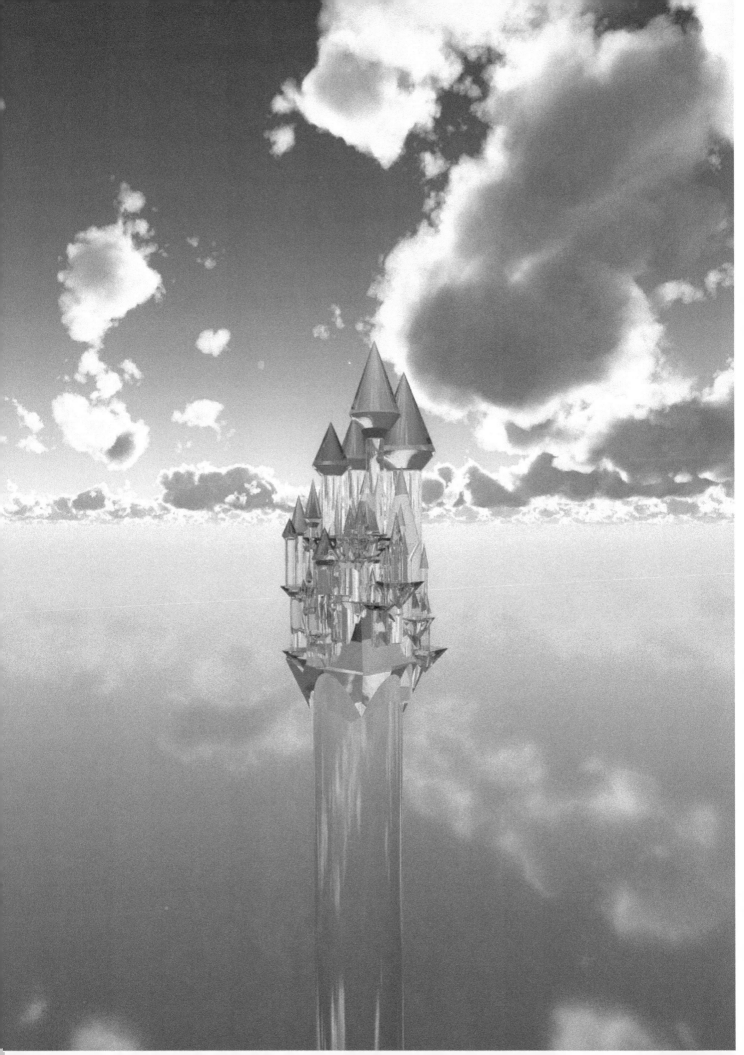

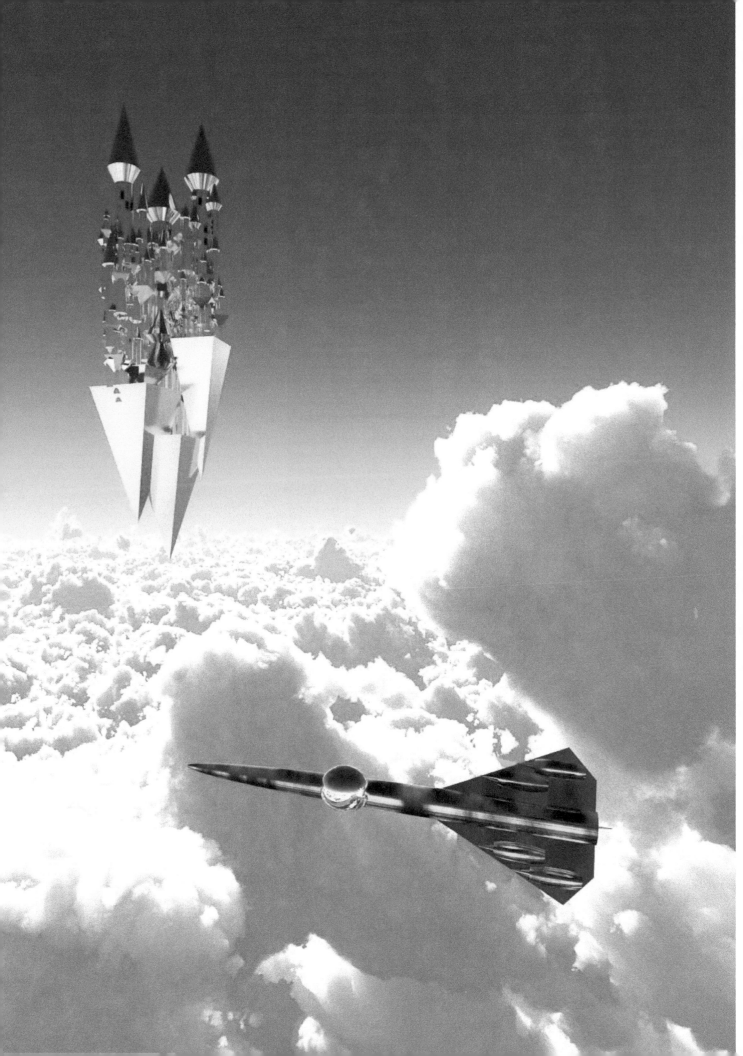

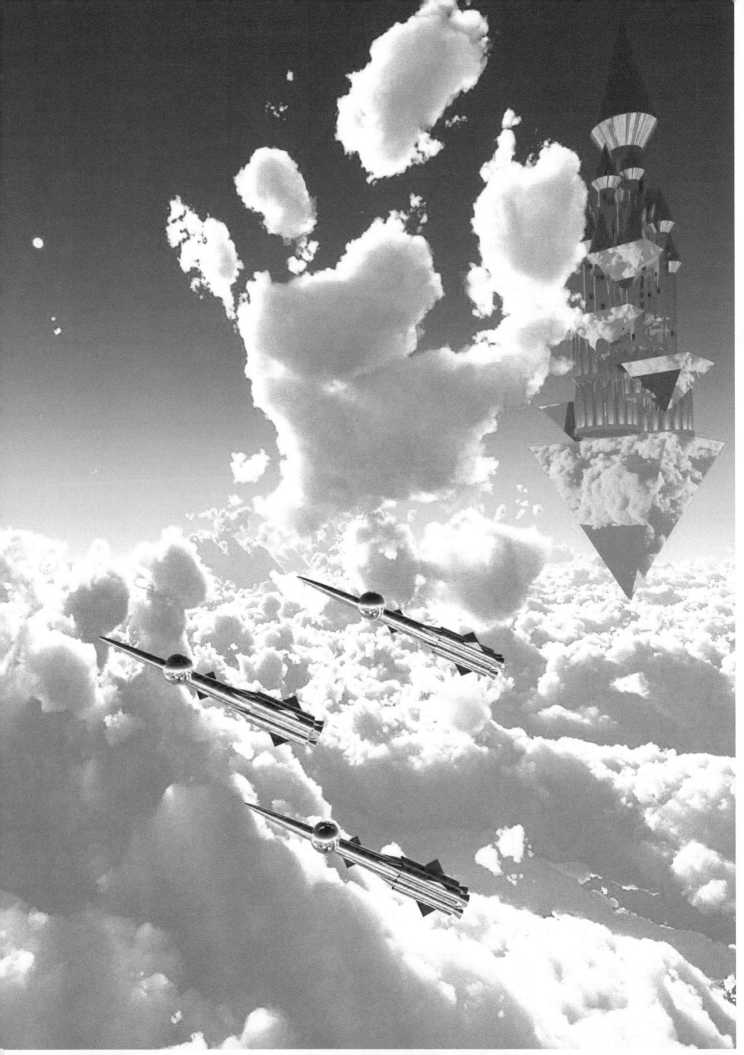

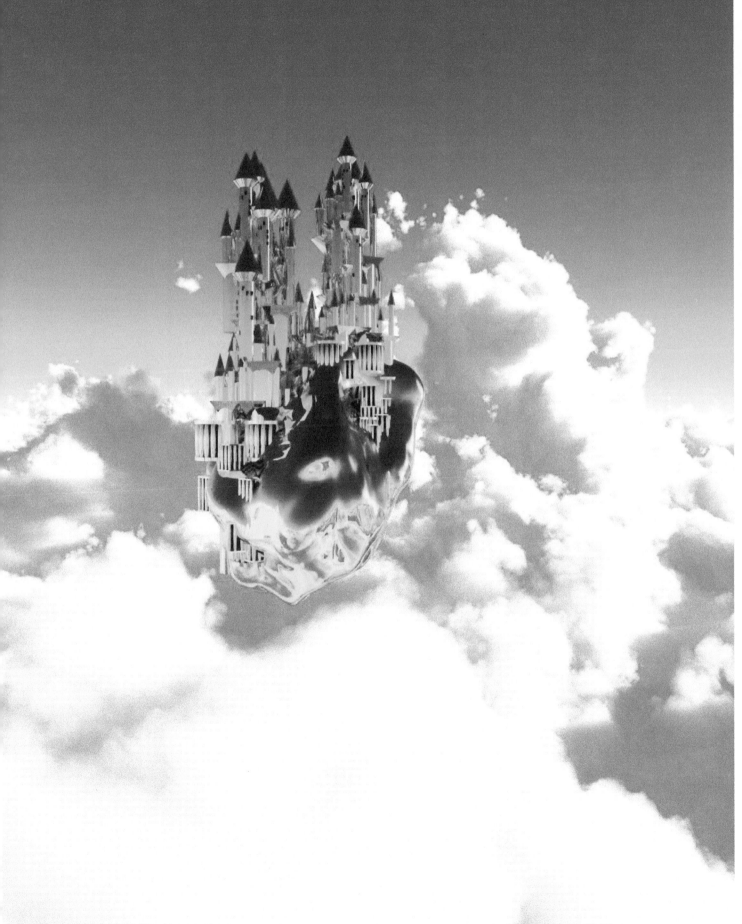

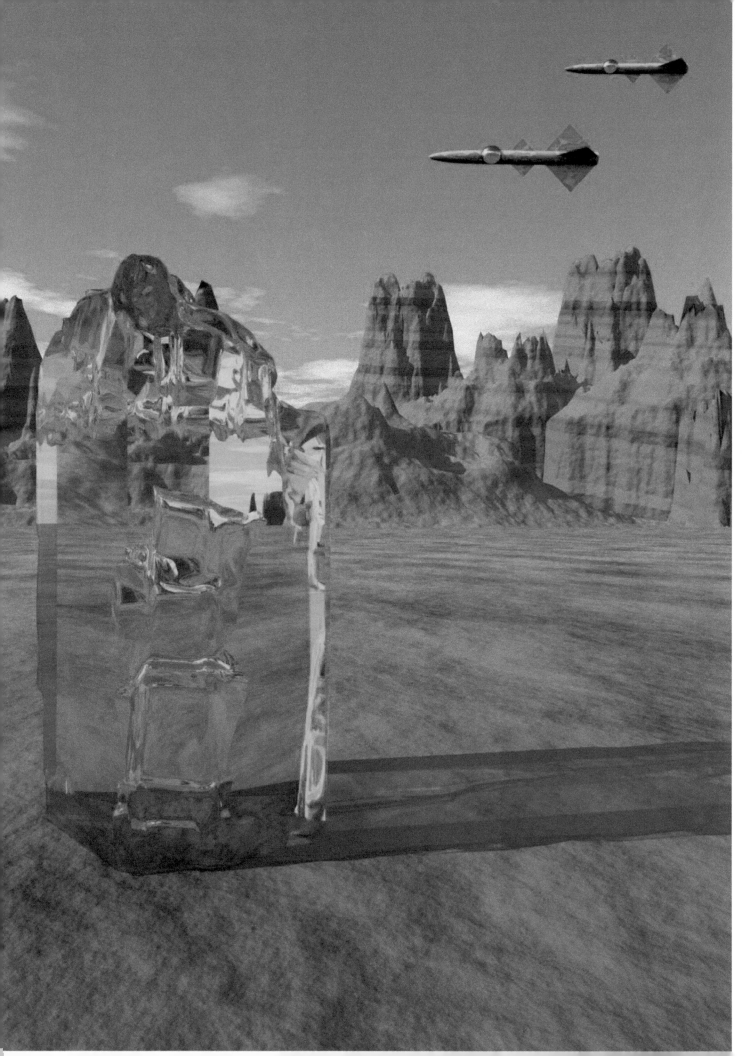

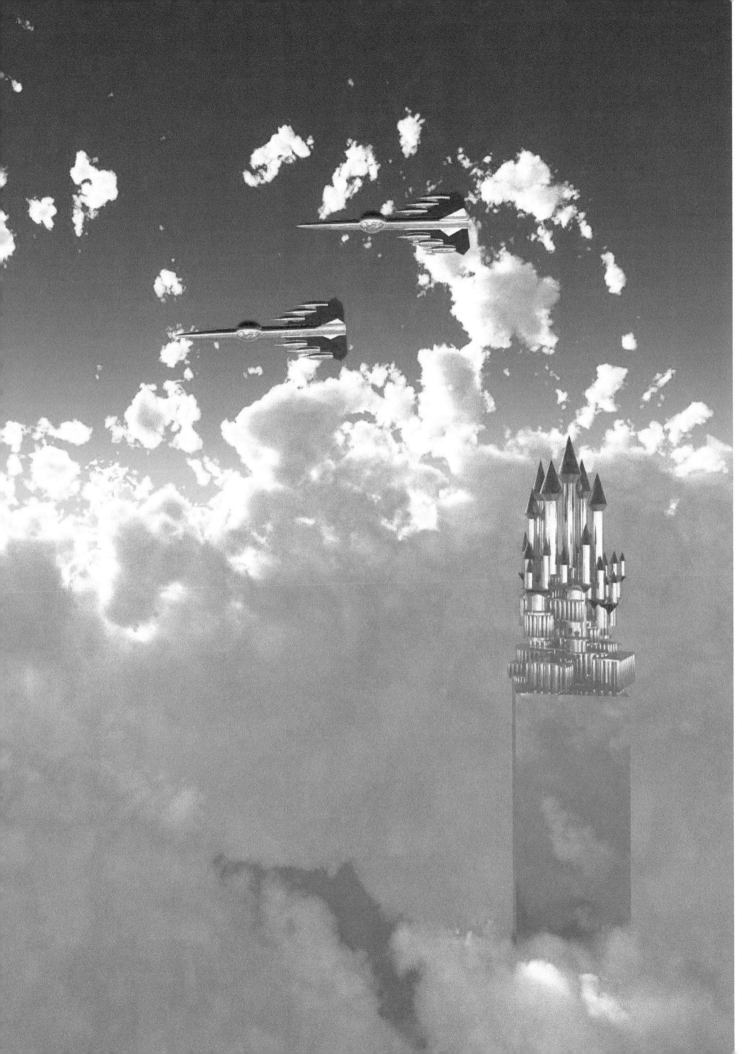

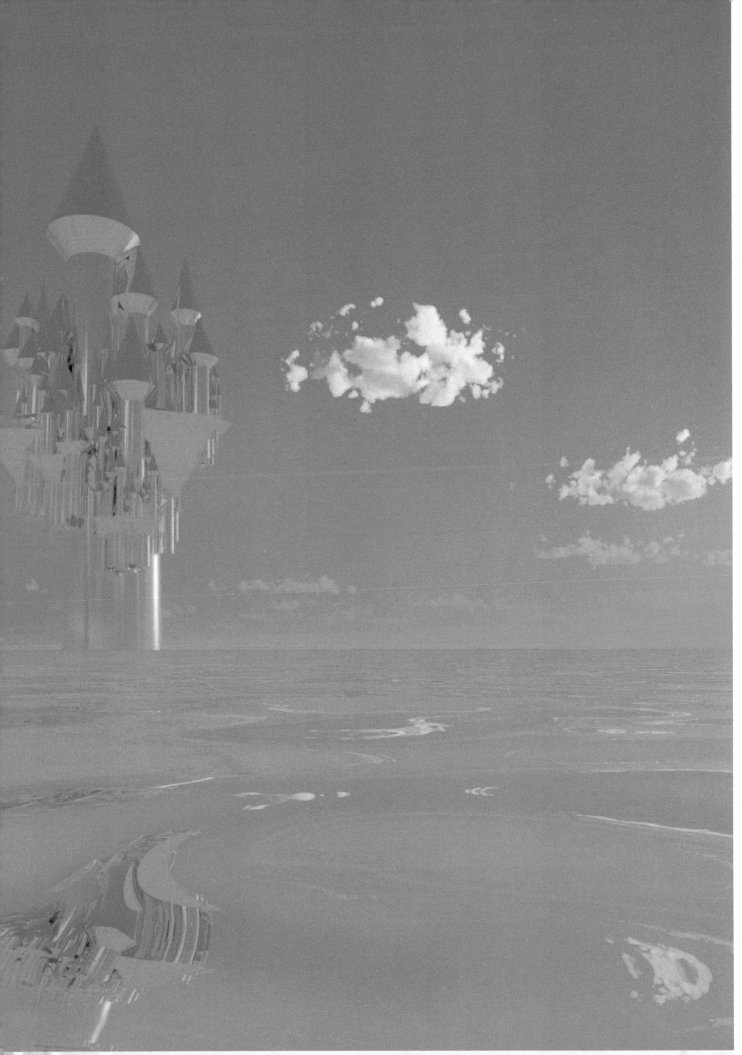

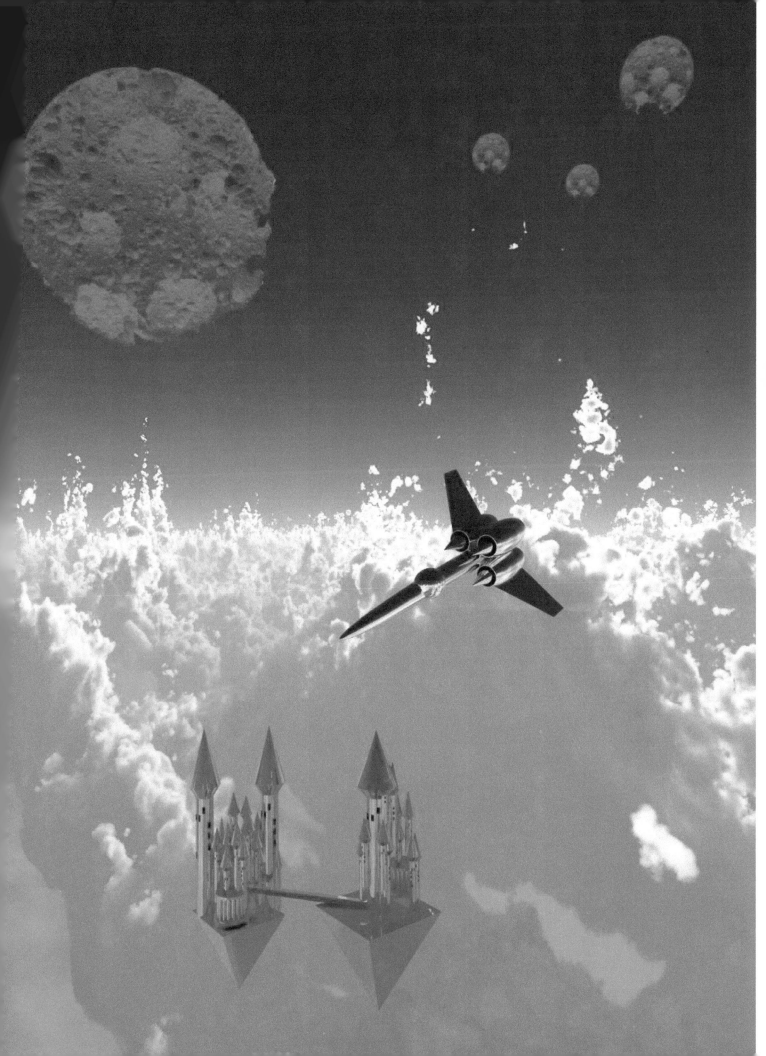

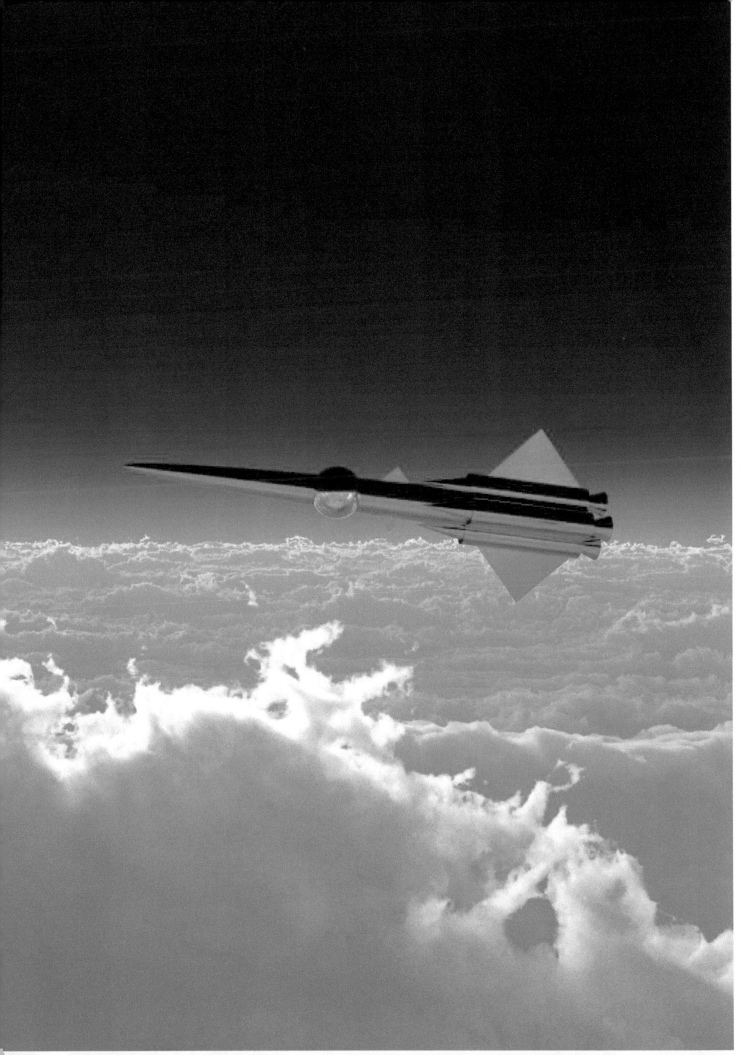

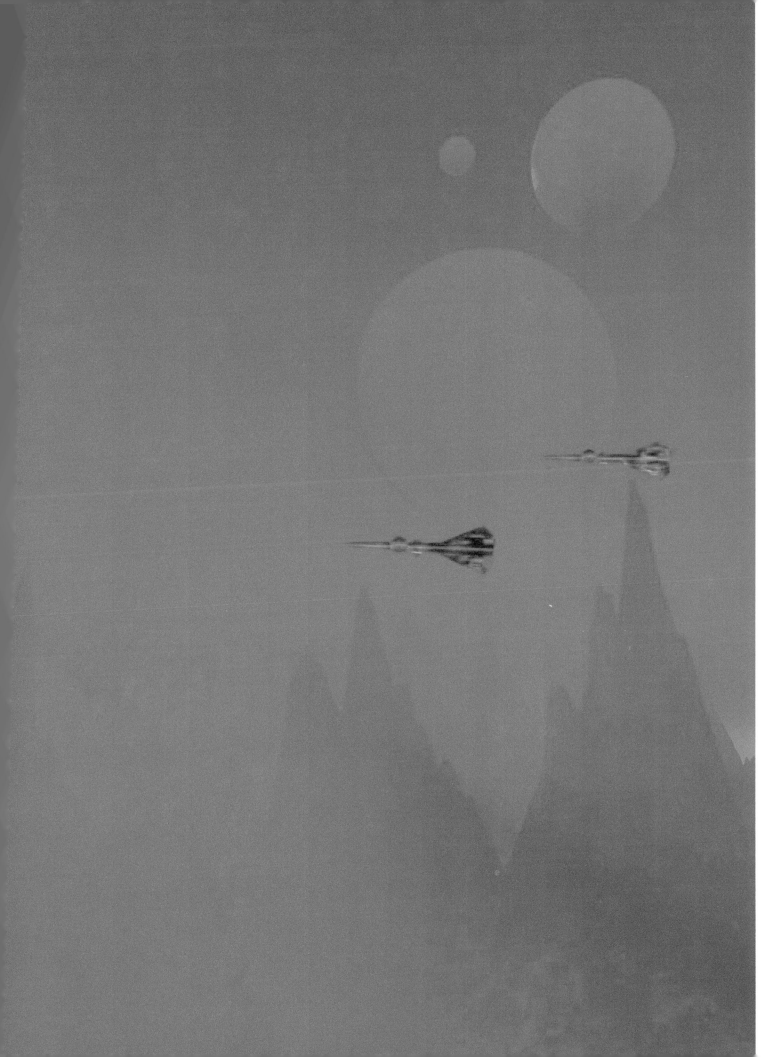

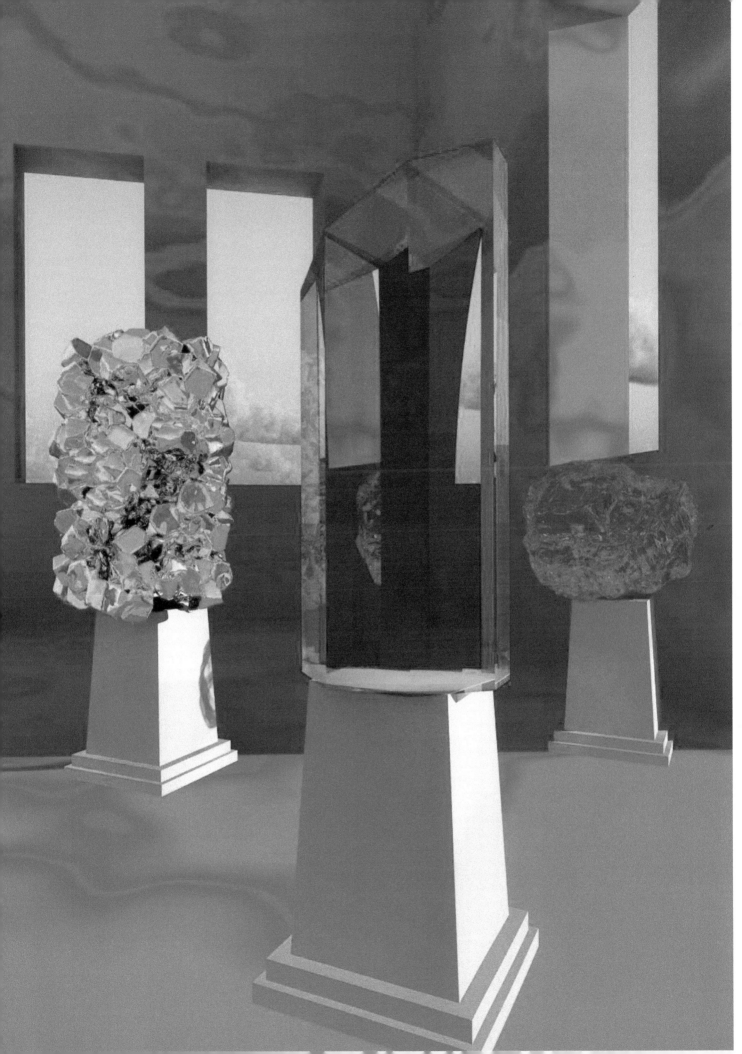

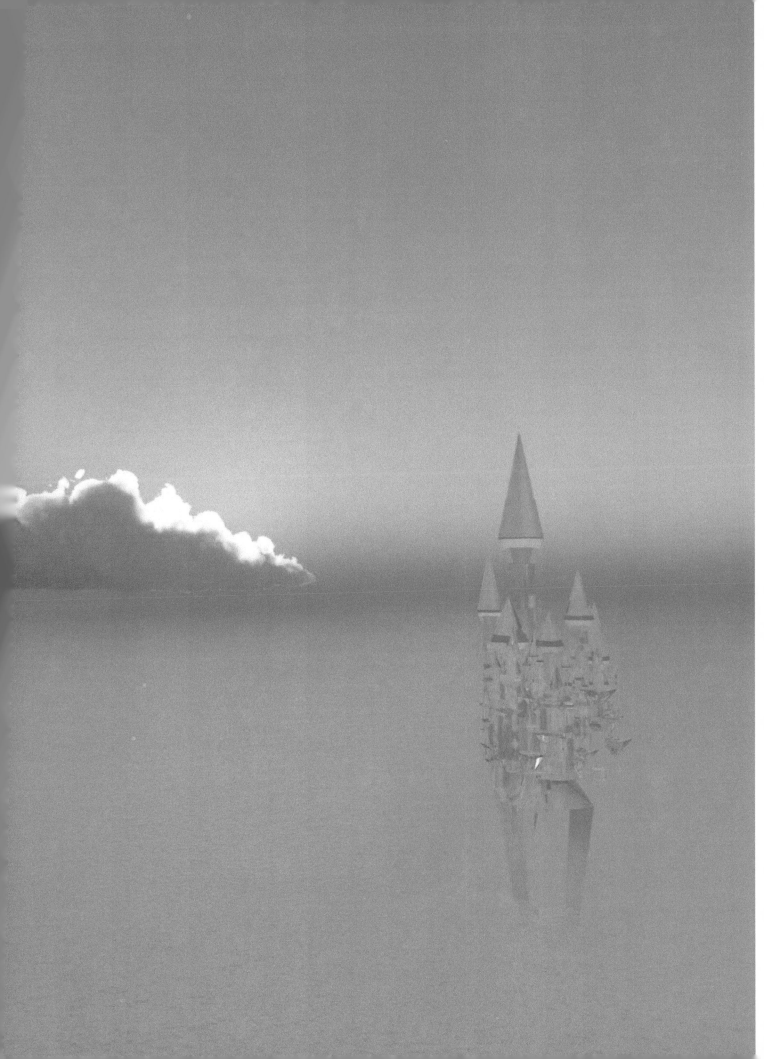

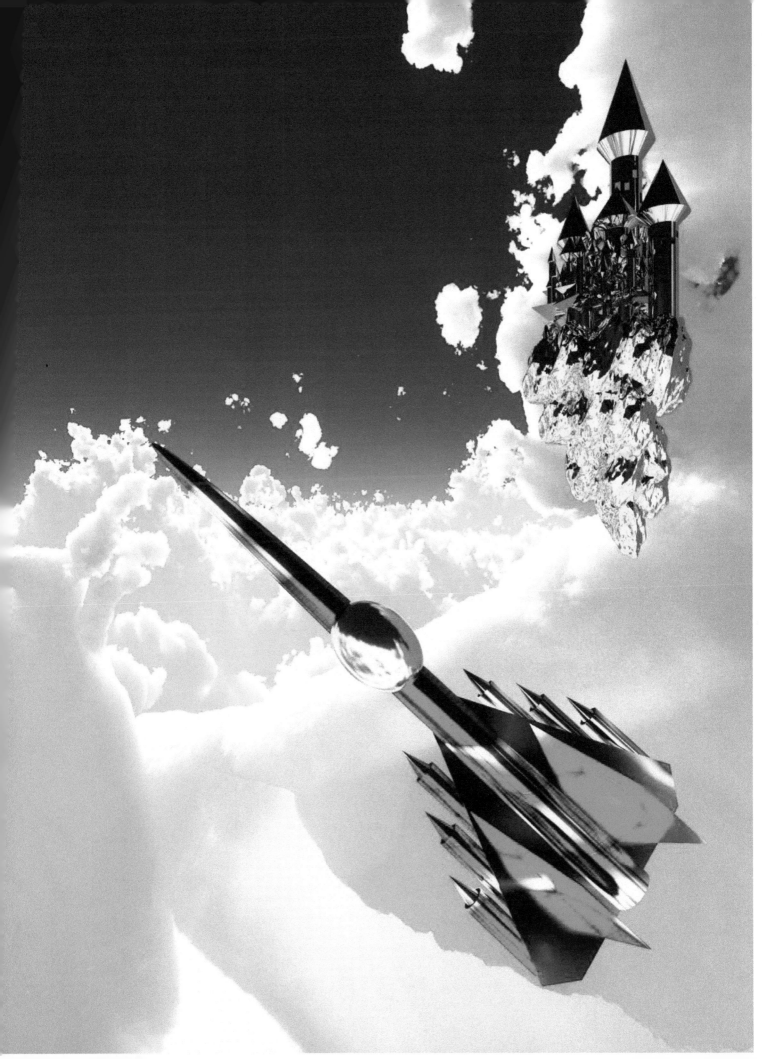

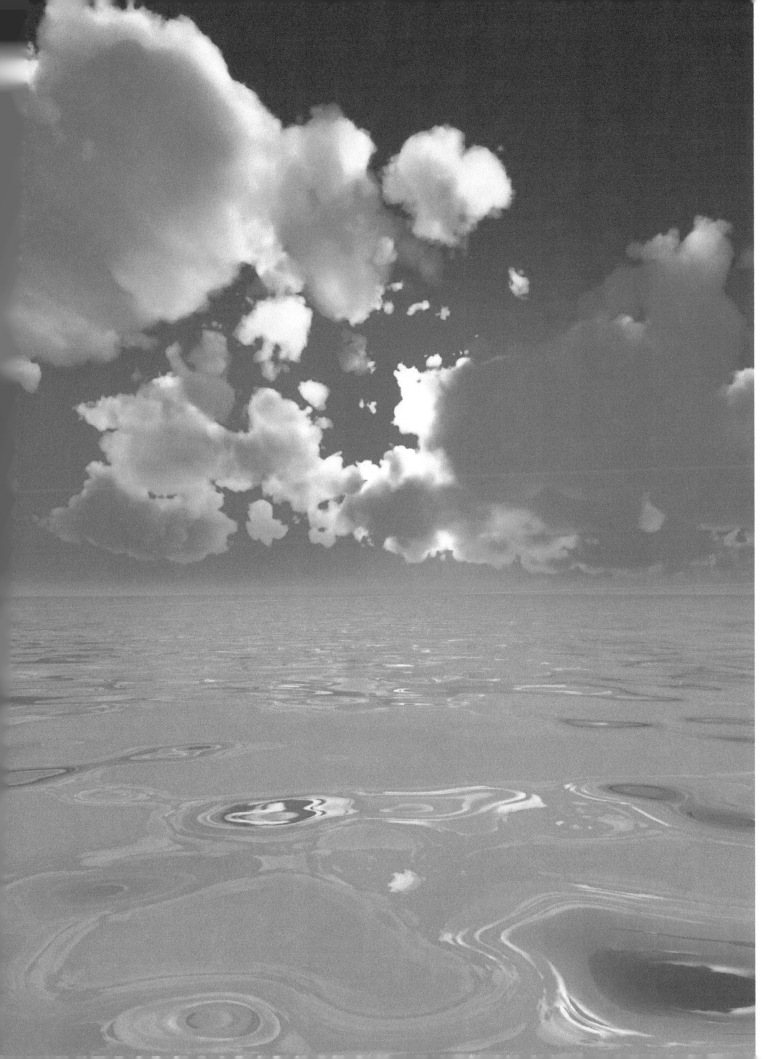

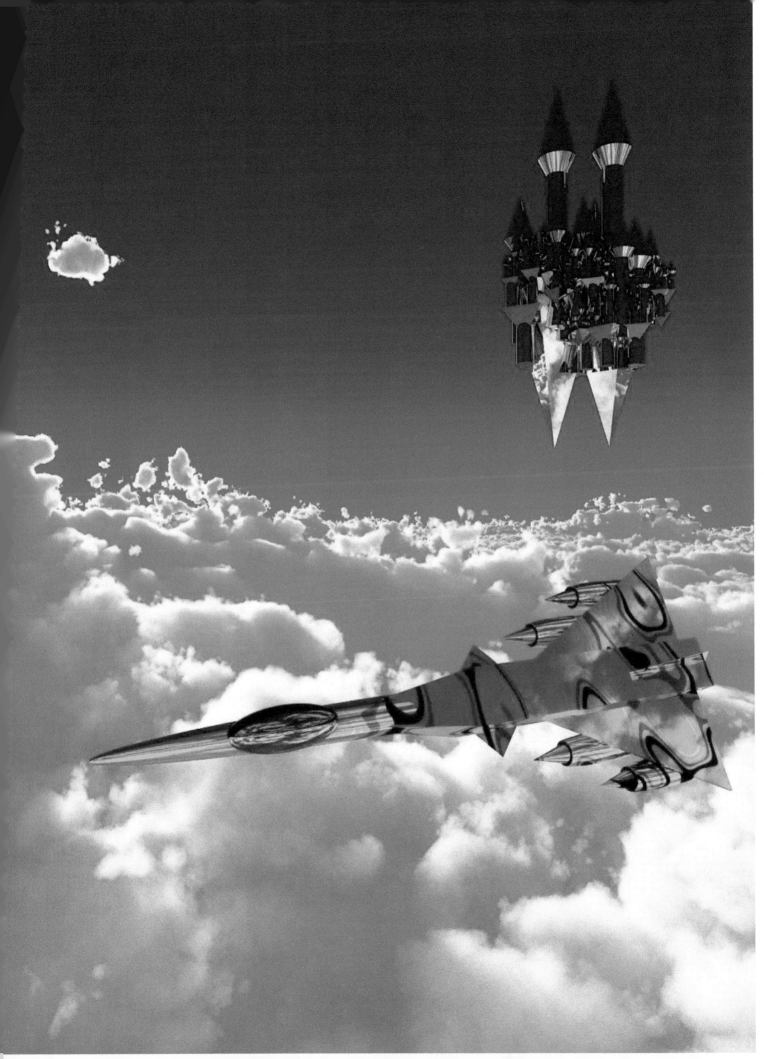

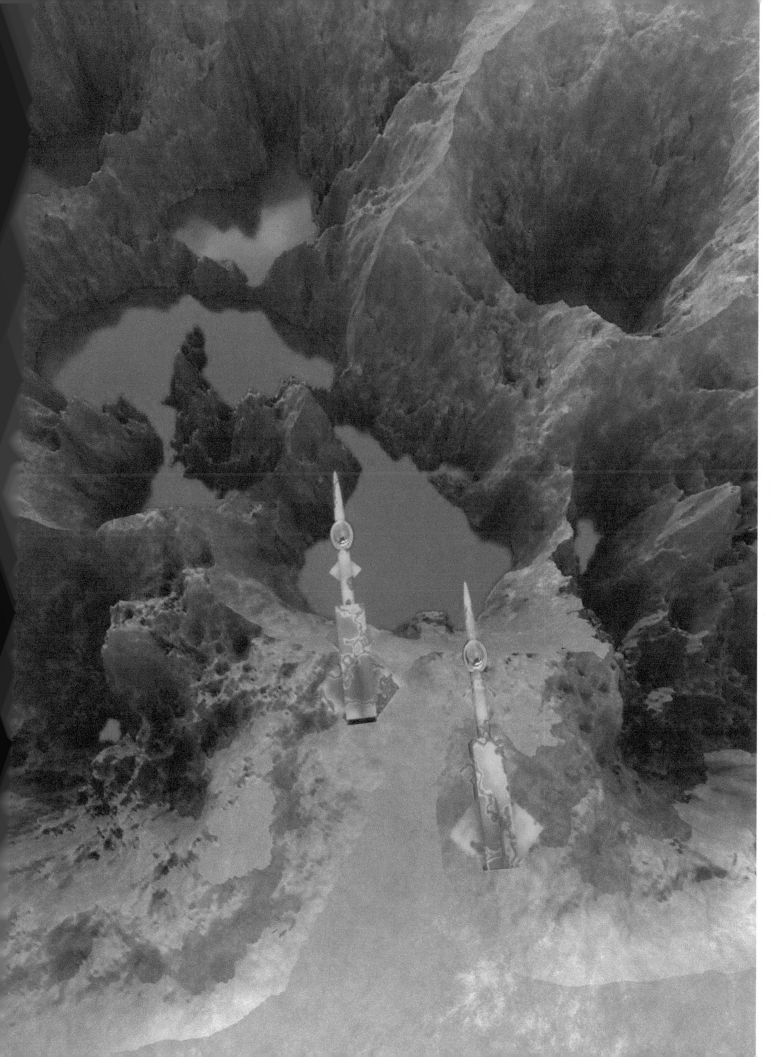

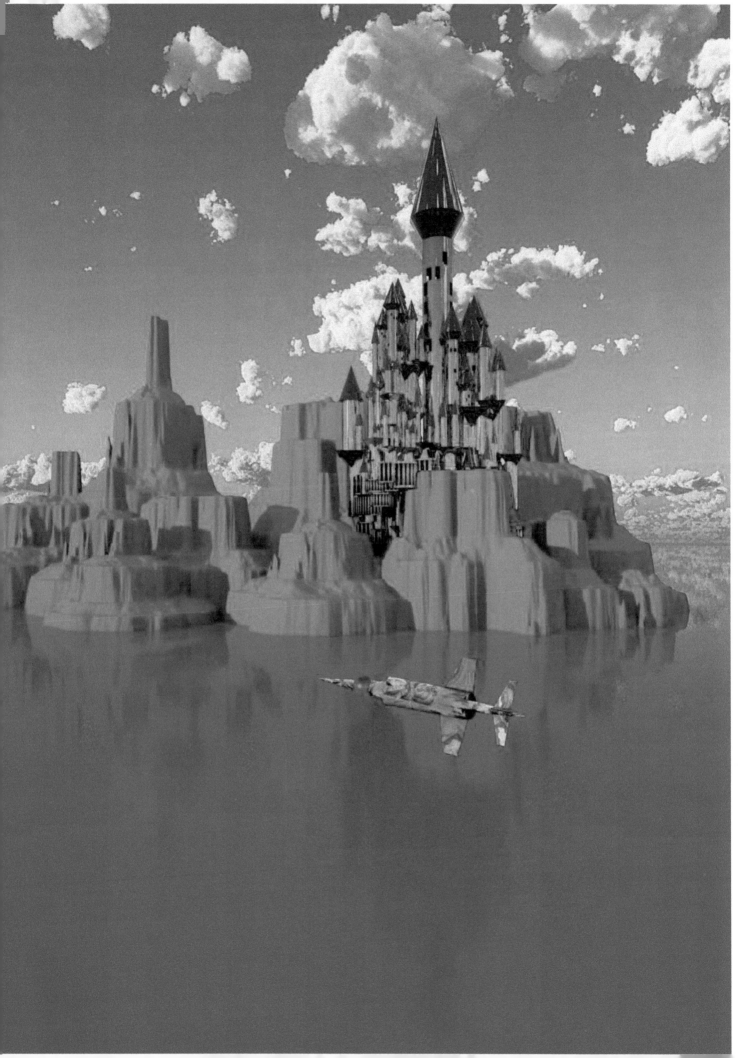

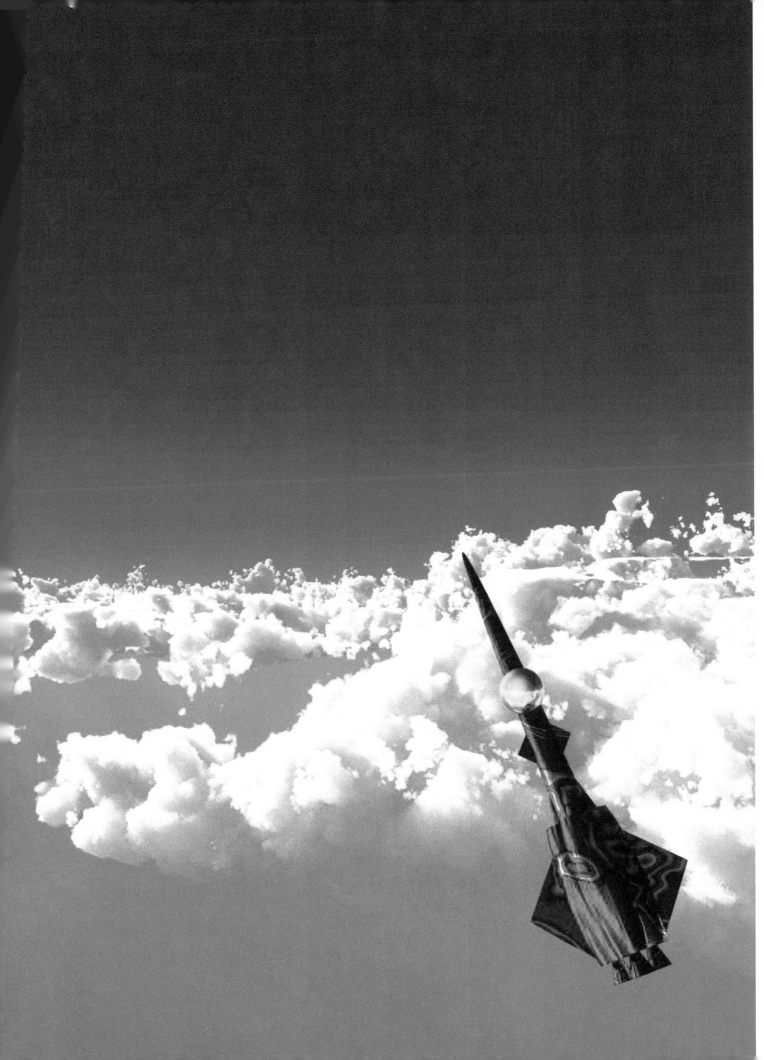

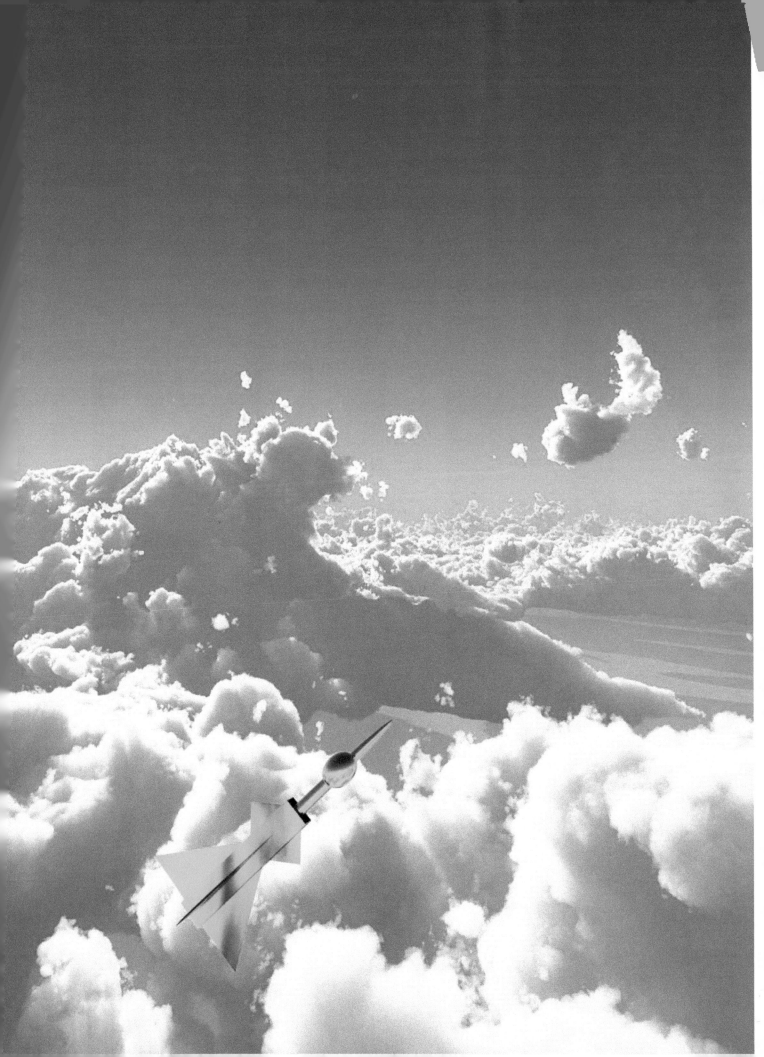

Find out more about Tim Gibson and King Tiger Books at:

https://kingtigerbooks.com/

https://www.facebook.com/kingtigerbooks/

Look for these books at your favorite on-line retailer:

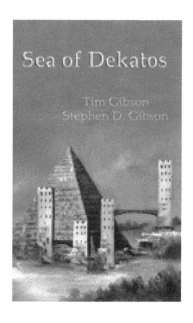

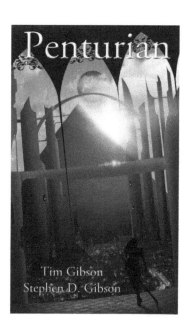